D0245663

THE ULTIMATE HERESY

THE AUTHOR

JOHN SEYMOUR is well known for his pioneering work in the thinking, writing and practice of self-sufficiency and organic farming. He was educated in England and Switzerland. He studied at an agricultural college in Kent, and has worked on various farms throughout his life. He spent ten years in Africa, where he managed a sheep farm; then, with his wife Sally he successfully ran a self-sufficient smallholding in Suffolk. After eight years they moved to Wales to a sixty-acre farm which became a school in the arts of self-sufficiency.

He now combines writing, travelling and lecturing with farming a smallholding in Ireland. He is the author of *Fat of the Land, Self-Sufficiency, The Forgotten Arts* and numerous other books. His six-part series *Far from Paradise* was shown on BBC1 in 1986.

The Ultimate Heresy

John Seymour

GREEN BOOKS

First published in 1989 by
Green Books
Ford House, Hartland
Bideford, Devon EX39 6EE

Typeset in Baskerville 11/13pt by
Computype, Exeter

Printed by Hartnolls,
Victoria Square
Bodmin, Cornwall

British Library Cataloguing
Seymour, John, *1914 –*
The ultimate heresy.
1. Environment. Effect of man.
I. Title.
304.2'8
ISBN 1-870098-24-2

Contents

Preface

THIS BOOK IS AN attempt to delineate the history of mankind's*
attitude to the rest of nature. In using the term 'the rest of
nature' I am anticipating the whole argument of the book, for
the Ultimate Heresy of the title, and the heresy that is likely to
damn us to ultimate extinction if we persist in it, is the belief
that we are apart from Nature and not a part of it. If we cannot
rid ourselves of this belief, and quickly, then we will not have a
very long tenure on this planet.

We are part of Nature. That is the primary condition of our
existence. And only when we recognise this will we awake
from the evil dream that has led us down the path of self-
destruction for the last two or three hundred years. That is the
dream that we, mankind, can 'conquer nature'. For only when
we abandon this dream will we realise again that *you cannot
conquer something of which you are a part.*

If we consider human history from just one point of view –
from the point of view of the attitude of humans to the rest of

---

*I use the word mankind in the generic sense – to mean the whole of
our species. Nothing sexist is intended in this. I am well aware that
the female half of our species is the more important component –
besides being far less prone than the male to fall into the heresy
under discussion.

creation – we come up against a strange paradox. This is that when people believed, because of their various religions, that they were *not* part of Nature they behaved as if they were. Only since most people have believed, rightly or wrongly, that they are descended from the ancestors of monkeys – i.e. that they *are* part of Nature just as much as any other animals or plants or other living things are, they have behaved as if they are *not* part of Nature and they feel they have a perfect right to exploit and use the rest of Nature for their own selfish ends. The medieval Christian, for example, believed that he was created quite separately from all other animals and plants upon this planet. And yet he believed in a way that indicates that *in his heart* he knew that he was just a creature like all the others, that he must not be too arrogant or destructive, and that he must just play his due part in the dance of Life upon this planet. The modern businessman however, despite the fact that if he thinks at all he thinks he is only another kind of monkey, behaves as if he is quite apart from, and above, all other living things and can do with them exactly what he likes. If it suits him to exterminate another species – or a thousand other species – he will do so without any compunction at all.

Now whatever we believe in, or whatever we don't believe in, we have got to accept that there is some force or tendency in this Universe that is working towards ever greater complexity. Astrophysicists tell us that there was a time when energy and matter did not exist. Now they do exist. We know, from studying the rocks of our own planet, that there was a time when life did not exist – here at least. Now it does exist. At first it was simple and unicellular. Then it became more complex and multicellular. At first it was unintelligent. Then intelligent life forms developed. At first intelligent forms were non-self-aware. Then they became self-aware. It may be anthropocentric to suppose that the creature we have so immodestly named *Homo sapiens* stands at the summit of Life on this planet. But most of us do assume it just the same. We are incontrovertibly more *complex* at least than the other forms of life. It may be Life-centred to suppose that living things are higher in some way than non-living matter. What – a slug is a higher organism than Mount Everest? Mount Everest without the life on it that is? Well, as a living thing myself I must believe so. As a human I must assume that humanity is 'higher' in some way than slugs, living though they undoubtedly are.

And I must recognise that there is some tendency in the Universe that has evolved/created greater complexity out of the less complex. I *know* that non-living matter has been transformed into living matter because I have seen it happening. I have watched the living lichens eating into the non-living rock and turning their substance into living matter.

So I *know* that there is a tendency in this Universe to turn non-matter into matter, simple atoms into complex molecules, non-living materials into living material, unicellular creatures into multicellular ones, non-intelligent creatures into intelligent ones. I know it because it has happened.

Now humans have for long recognised that there is this tendency that makes for greater complexity – a higher degree of organisation – greater beauty if you like – in the Universe, but they have found it very difficult to contemplate such an abstraction as a . . . *tendency*. So they have anthropomorphised the concept. They have clothed this abstraction in the trappings of humankind. They have imagined the tendency that has made something out of nothing as a God, or Goddess, or a multiplicity of Goddesses and Gods.

And why not? If it helps us to understand the tendency that drives the Universe to ever greater complexity and beauty – the *Life Force* as some have called it – then why not do it? Maybe other sentient creatures throughout the Universe do the same.

3

A sluggish theologian said 'It's odd
That anyone as sensible as God
Who made we slugs in His own image can
Put up with this disgusting creature Man.'

Maybe we all have to create God in our own image to understand It/Her/Him.

And from the beginning of recorded history people have divined that true happiness and well-being depend upon something they have called 'obeying the will of God'. In more modern terms a man (writing under the name Tomot Om, in a little book called in English *On the Side of Life*) has called it working in accordance with the aims of the Life Force. If we think of it most of us will realise that happiness does depend upon just this. So then it is very important to discover what *are* the aims of the Life Force – what is, in theological language then, the will of God?

And here I believe we must call on something other than our own pure intelligence. It has been surmised that we have, in our brains, not only pure intelligence but something else as well. Call it intuition, or instinct (it is more than just that), or revelation – call it what you like but we all (or most of us) know we have got it. We Westerners have suppressed it for too long now but we still have it. And possibly we must revive it, or dig it up again, if we wish to discover what is the true reason for our being here on this planet at all. It is very important that we should arrive at the right answer.

CHAPTER ONE

The Palaeolithic View
of Nature

*Hear me, four quarters of the world – a relative I am. Give me the
strength to walk the soft earth, a relative to all that is.*
Oglala Sioux prayer from *Black Elk Speaks*.

WHEN JOSEPH THE BUSHMAN and I used to walk through the
veld, he walked in front of me and I watched him. I tried
to imitate him. When I walk through the woods on my own
farm I break off any small branches that impede me, and if I
carry a slasher, as I often do, I slash brambles that are
straggling over the path so as to open the way.

Joseph never broke any small branch off. He moved
through the bush as a fish swims in water – he was part of it. As
he walked he disturbed nothing. And I noticed that even when
Joseph moved along paths that he moved along every
day – such as the one which led from his grass hut to the sheep
kraal in which the flock he was in charge of spent every night –
he still disturbed nothing. A white man or a Bantu (a member
of the 'more advanced' black East and South African race)
would have slashed back the bushes and made a proper path.
This course of action never occurred to Joseph.

Joseph was a 'tame' Bushman. He had been captured and
used as a slave by an Afrikaans family when he was a little boy.

5

He therefore spoke Afrikaans and as I knew the rudiments of this language I was able to talk with him. In any case, as many a white man who has made friends with a Bushman has found before me, it is hardly necessary to know the same language as a Bushman to converse with him. The members of this race have a quite uncanny way of making their thoughts known to you, and of understanding what you are trying to say.

Joseph was infinitely quicker-witted than I am. He divined things – I had to work them out. Officially, I don't believe in many of the things that some young Western people believe in today. For example I don't believe in telepathy, yet I swear we used to converse with never a word being uttered. In any case, he never let me finish a sentence. As soon as I opened my mouth to utter some of my halting Afrikaans, Joseph would cut me short and answer whatever it was that I had been trying to ask.

I have been hunting many times with Joseph. Joseph was employed as a shepherd on my boss's farm. This meant that he was in charge of a flock of between three and four hundred sheep. He put these sheep away in a fenced *kraal* every night, had the sheep counted out of the *kraal* by a white man (generally me) in the morning, and then wandered off into the veld with them, trying to keep them away from the flocks of other shepherds (there were six flocks on the farm), and guarding them from wild beasts, of which there were plenty.

But some mornings Joseph used to take his sheep away into the hot dry bush country and hand them over to his wife. She was just as good a shepherd as he was. He would then go to a certain bush – a *wag-n-bietjie* bush ('wait-a-bit' – if you touched against it you had to wait a bit because its needle-sharp thorns caught hold of you), and he would thrust his arm into it and pull out the head of an assegai – throwing spear. The head had no shaft: Joseph would cut a shaft for it when he got further into the bush. 'Natives' were not allowed to own spears in South West Africa.

Joseph and I used to go hunting for the mighty and beautiful gemsbok or oryx. At first I used to take my rifle. Joseph *always* knew where the buck were most likely to be. When we were searching for gemsbok Joseph would stop occasionally, look around, sniff the air, and change direction. He couldn't really have smelled anything – we were still miles from the animals and perhaps up-wind – but he never failed to find the antelope. The veld was vast; the buck were few. It was like looking for a needle in a haystack. But Joseph *never failed*. Maybe I learned something of the art from him, for I developed what other people considered to be an uncanny aptitude for finding game.

I have read about the 'left and right brain' theory, and it immediately made sense to me, not so much because of the division of the brain into a left and right lobe, one lobe being responsible for one sort of activity and the other for another, but because I had already divined that there are two parts of my brain – the part I *think* with and the part I *feel* with. I know that the part I *think* with (whether it's left or right, all over or in the middle, I don't give a damn) is almost completely dominant over the part I *feel* with. I am a thinking animal, not a feeling one. Joseph *felt* as much as he thought. The survival of the Bushmen, a Palaeolithic people living in one of the most hostile environments in the world depends entirely on their ability to feel and to divine things. A white man, lost in the Namib Desert, even with a rifle, dies very quickly. Admittedly the Bushman starts with a physical advantage, being able to walk sixty miles in twenty-four hours with no water – but it is the capacity to feel that really enables him to survive.

I can only realise some of the potential of the right lobe of my brain (for convenience sake I will assume the geographical explanation) by anaesthetising the left. I can do this with alcohol or with a mushroom of the *Psilocybin* genus (by far the more effective and less damaging to the health).

Anaesthetising the left lobe, or at least partially disabling it, leaves me unbalanced so that although I achieve great insights by getting drunk and by eating mushrooms, I cannot at the time subject these insights to the scrutiny of the left lobe, nor can I take any effective action. Joseph, all the time and without recourse to any drugs, had the full use of his right lobe as well as of his left.

I also believe that we 'white men', after developing our left lobes to unprecedented heights, have lost to differing degrees the use of our right lobes. We think supremely, but we cannot feel. We can no longer *divine* things. Sir Winston Churchill managed to feel and divine quite a lot, by the simple expedient of having a flask of whisky constantly beside him and having recourse to it pretty often. He felt and divined enough to out-feel and out-divine Hitler, who was a teetotaller. But he was one of those unusual people who are able to make pretty good use of their left lobes while at least getting some use out of their right lobes too. Joseph the Bushman could do this and better.

Ah then – if they are so intelligent why have the Bushmen not invented the atomic bomb? They have been living exactly the way they live now since their ancestors were painting animals in caves a quarter of a million years ago and all they have succeeded in inventing is the bow and poisoned arrow, and they had those then. They have invented *nothing* in a quarter of a million years. Even the assegai that Joseph unlawfully owned was a borrowing from the Bantu. No Bushman ever smelted iron.

The reasons why Palaeolithic Man never invented the atomic bomb are, firstly, the very caste of character that made Joseph forbear to break off a twig on the path between his hut and the sheep *kraal*, and secondly the fact that their left lobes were never developed to great heights at the expense of their right lobes.

They felt, and the few survivors like Joseph still feel, entirely a part of the rest of Nature. It would never have occurred to Joseph, for one second, that he was 'above' Nature. He felt a part of it exactly as he felt that the jackal and the lion were part of it. He was a partner in it with them. Joseph told me many stories, and I have read others, written down by one of the very few missionaries who ever managed to master the extraordinary khoi-san language which is half made up of clicks, of the legends of the Bush people. It is obvious from these that there is no difference in the minds of the story tellers between Man and the rest of Nature. The animals were people too – the people animals, and *all* were part of the great stream of Life. Joseph was interested in the stars, and looked upon them too as his brothers and sisters. We read that the true Australians have these characteristics too.

And how then could he fling his assegai into the flank of the antelopes as I have seen him do? *For the very reason* that he knew that he, Joseph, was a part of nature – and had to play his part in Nature. The Bushmen were carnivores. The men who painted the cave paintings at Altimara were carnivores too. Do not many of these paintings depict men throwing spears into large animals – or shooting at them with bows and arrows? I think that Joseph apologised in his heart to his brother the gemsbok as he flung the spear. Though he would probably not have put the prayer into words, it might have run something like this: 'The life force ordains that your kind shall crop the grass after the rains and munch the tsava melons – and nibble the dry grey leaves of the small bushes in the dry season, and dig up corms with your sharp hooves and eat them to get water during the nine months of drought. You destroy these things so that they shall become part of a higher form of life, and the Life Force ordains that I shall kill you, my Brother, and partake of your flesh, so that I can live too. I shall die too; maybe a lion will eat me, maybe when I am old my children will leave me inside a little thorn pen, with a few ostrich shells full of water

9

and a little food, with my wife who is my companion, and we shall die as most Bushmen die, and be reintegrated with the Nature of our land.'

I have heard that old 'wild' Bushmen and women, when thus left behind by the tribe in its ceaseless searchings across the desert because the old people can no longer keep up, compose themselves to their desertion and death with happy smiles and cheerful hearts. Parting with their younger relations is a joyful occasion, and the night before the younger people leave them is spent in singing and dancing.

The position might be held that all of Life should be a preparation to meet death. Among most white people, death is dreaded with horror and loathing – even by Christians, who affect to believe that it leads to Paradise. People are terrified of it. It is a shadow that hangs over humans during all of their lives except in their early childhood before they know what it is. Most Westerners manage to forget death for much of their time on Earth by diverting themselves with constant activities, lusts, appetites and the satisfying of them, and with what Aldous Huxley called tumescence and detumescence. With lust for power, and power struggles, and endless restless activity and movement and opiates of a thousand kinds, Mankind forgets death. Wars and preparations for wars are of course examples of this frantic search for anything that will divert our thoughts from death. Consider the stink of our bodies as we lie rotting in the coffin. Bodies, I am told, sit up violently owing to spontaneous contraction of the muscles, and their faces contort horrifically as they are slid coffinless, into the fires of the incinerator. So no matter how we are disposed of, death is horrible.

Paradoxically it is this horror of death that leads Western Man to have the death-wish, and leads him to invent things like the atomic bomb. I spent years in the company of Joseph – he was by far the best friend I ever had and I am quite sure that he had no fear of death whatever – and no death wish: the thought of death just did not bother him at all.

Joseph and I sat on the ground a few yards away from a dead donkey one cold and moonless night, he with his spear and my shotgun, me with a seven millimetre Mauser rifle. We had no protection of any kind, it was nearly pitch dark, and we had no torch. We knew that the donkey (one of five) had been killed by a pride of three lions. Joseph knew every single detail about those three lions – merely from studying their footprints. We knew the lions would come back to their kill. No white man, unless he was with a man like Joseph and had implicit faith in him, or else was slightly mad, would have sat on the open ground, with no protection around him – neither in front nor on the sides nor behind – on a pitch dark night waiting for a lion. A rifle is a fine weapon but useless if you can't see what you are trying to shoot. A lion, like a cat, can see in the dark. One backward stroke of a lion's hind foot will rip a man's guts out. We killed a lion that night, at exactly three yards' range, and I well remember how Joseph leapt up, after the bullet had gone into its brain, and shouted: 'A man with a good heart need fear nothing!' He took it for granted that his heart was good – but he was less sure about the white man's.

The next day Joseph and I walked very quickly thirty miles over the trackless veld following the other two lions. The trio had been doing a lot of damage to my employer's stock so I wanted to kill them too. To watch Joseph tracking was weird. He just walked flat out, in his effortless way, casting his eyes occasionally at the ground but obviously noticing every detail of Nature around him – missing nothing – and yet never losing the spoor or trail of the animals. Several times I tried him out by asking how he knew we were still on the spoor. At first he would look at me as you would look at a man who affected not to be able to see a bus a yard away from him. What – could it be *possible* that I had not noticed that that leaf there had been pressed into the ground an hour ago – or that that tiny pebble

11

had been turned over about the same time. (The bottom of it had a slightly different shade to the sun-roasted top.) And look, good God – there is the actual imprint of one of the lobes of the she-lion's left hind foot in that tiny pocket of soil on the bare limestone. Look – that's the foot that – I told you – had an old cut in it, now healed up! And he looked at me hard, with a puzzled look – could it be *possible* I was *that* blind . . . ?

After a time he ceased to look at me with amazement. He just realised that, no matter how well we got on together, I was of a different species and as blind as a bat. He would just contemptuously throw his hand in the direction of the really *obvious* lion footprint, where such existed, in a patch of bare dust where you could have seen a ghost's spoor, just to reassure me that we were still on the right track.

We came to where the lions had drunk water at a trough near a farmhouse. Their footprints were deep in the wet mud by the water-trough. We had followed them, walking flat out, for thirty miles. Joseph knew exactly how long ago they had been there by a hundred signs that were invisible to me and we decided that they were gaining on us and that anyway, it was time we went home. We would never catch up with the lions.

Troopers of the South West African Police used to employ Bushmen as trackers and I have heard them say, many times, that try as they would they could never understand how Bushmen manage to follow an apparently invisible spoor and that, try as they would, the most intelligent of white men was still incapable of learning the art.

Of course, even for the purposes of the Life Force, the Early Stone Age is inferior in a hundred ways to the Industrial Age or the Age of Technology. The Bushmen survived the impact of the Neolithic and Bronze and Iron Age tribes that came sweeping down through Africa – the Bantu people – though only just. But now that the white man has arrived the outlook is terribly bleak. I was shown, at the old police fort at Tsumeb, a copy of the edict posted up in German (before the South

12

Africans marched in in the First World War, South West Africa was a German colony) naming the animals that they classed as vermin, meaning that they could be shot without a licence and at any season. Bushmen were about halfway down the list. Before the First World War there was a great trade in Bushmen skulls and skeletons. These used to be sent to Europe to be studied by anthropologists, or exhibited in anthropological exhibitions. Hunters used to shoot every Bushman, man, woman or child they could find, lay the bodies near ant-hills so that they would be picked clean before the jackals spoiled the bones, and then packed them in sacks and sent them down to Walvis Bay to be shipped to Europe. There is a splendid account in *Twenty-five Years in a Wagon* by Andrew Anderson of how the author found a Boer family in Natal, the man of which had just shot a Bushman and captured his family. The family were locked up in a hut while the Boer husband and wife debated whether it would be better to shoot them or retain them as slaves. The woman wanted the first course to be followed – the man the second. Young Bushmen girls were very pretty.

In our own day white people are far more humane. I was told by several police troopers how, when the police came upon some Bushmen who were too gorged with meat to run away, they took them back and simply imprisoned them. It took them two or three weeks to die of claustrophobia. A 'wild' Bushman cannot endure, for more than a week or two, being confined in a cell. Of course *any* 'wild' Bushman can be arrested. Simply by existing he is committing many crimes. According to South African law it is illegal for him to carry arms – and he cannot exist without his bow and arrow. It is illegal for any 'native' to 'poach' game. Game is preserved for white people. Any policeman can arrest any 'wild' Bushman confident in the knowledge that the Bushman is breaking the law, and that he will die after a week or two in the cell thus making it unnecessary to bring any charges against him.

Of course Bushmen, in the past, occasionally hunted the white man's cattle. Well – the white men destroyed all the wild game on the huge areas of land that they grabbed and the cattle became the only animals left for people to eat.

More and more Bushmen now are spending more and more of their time working as servants on white men's farms. If the present trend continues, it will only be a decade or two before the Palaeolithic culture has disappeared entirely from the face of the planet.

I don't want to give the impression, by saying that the Bushmen have not suppressed the right lobes of their brains by developing the left ones, that they are incapable of reason, or, indeed, of very great intelligence. I have no doubt whatever that the Bushman is every bit as intelligent as Einstein was. I remember Clinton, my boss in South West Africa, describing to me how a Bushman boy slightly older than himself (that is about twelve) constructed with him a wind pump out of bits of wood that they cut out of the bushes of the veld. The windmill – like the hundreds of thousands of real pumping windmills all over the white-occupied parts of South Africa – worked perfectly and actually pumped water. Clinton said that it was his idea to make it but the Bushman boy did all the working out and construction of it. And Joseph was certainly the most intelligent man I have ever known.

Why then cannot the few remaining Palaeolithic men use their good intelligence to match the intelligence of the all-conquering white man and thus survive? Is it just because they don't want to fight? As long as they are allowed to they swim in Nature – they are Nature and feel this and have never believed for a millionth of a second that they are anything else. The white man wants to conquer Nature, and the Bushman, being a part of Nature must be conquered too – maybe a few will be retained in zoos, if they can survive these.

We could deduce from all this that Palaeolithic Man has indeed been passed over by the Life Force, and that he is

14

'meant' to fade away and leave the boundless veld free for men with rifles, Landrovers and barbed wire fences.

On the other hand – maybe this is a short-sighted view – maybe he is not 'meant' to fade away. Maybe Technological Man is 'meant' to develop sufficient restraint and humanity, sufficiently soon, to spare the Bushmen – and the wild tribes of Borneo, and the Australian Aborigines – and permit them to go on living their age-old existence in their age-old way. Maybe, too, *Homo extinctor* (as he should now be called, as he has proved totally unworthy of *sapiens*) – before he manages to destroy all other forms of life – will destroy himself and leave a few remnants of the Palaeolithic tribes still in existence. And as for survival – if only a few specimens of *H. extinctor* stay alive after the Holocaust, and a few members of the Bushman race, I know which I would put my money on. As a specimen, although a reluctant one, of *H. extinctor* I would far prefer the first scenario. It is *just* conceivable that it will be the real one and that after all we can *all* survive.

Now this chapter was to be about the relationship between Palaeolithic Man and the rest of Nature. I have tried to convey, mostly by anecdote, what is the attitude of the rest of Nature of the Namib Bushman. Of course Joseph was 'tame' and spoke Afrikaans, and was not a typical specimen, and yet I knew him long enough and intimately enough to have a very good idea of what a man who is a Bushman thought about things.

Many missionaries, and a few anthropologists, have tried to find out from the Bushmen what their ideas are about God. The Bushmen have told them various things. Certainly there is a consistency in the reports – the Bushmen quite definitely believe in a 'Great Spirit', although anthropologists generally write them off as 'animists': they worship special trees, water places, sticks and stones, the moon, jackals and other animals.

Joseph had heard all about the Calvinistic God when he was a slave boy with the Boer family. I don't know what on Earth he thought of *Him!* But he certainly had an idea of God of his own and, if we must give everything labels, I must say that he was a pantheist. He believed that God was in everything – everything was God. He merely used the Dutch word for God because he knew that was what we whites understood. But I know very well indeed that Joseph believed passionately in a Divine Force – the Life Force if you like – and that his particular belief gave significance to everything he did – everything he saw – and everything he believed in.

As for Joseph's attitude to what we white men were doing – I could only guess at most of that. I remember though, very vividly, once, when Clinton had a lot of gelignite left over from some blasting that we had done, and had asked me to get rid of it by blowing up some termite nests. Joseph saw me doing this, and expressed great distaste and disapproval at what I was doing.

Of course the termite, or white ant, does damage to the works of the white people. It consumes wood. We whites didn't know then, did we, about the essential part the termite plays in tropical ecology. For it breaks dead wood down into good compost which can immediately be taken back into the life cycle. In that dry climate it would otherwise just lie there for decades without rotting, or provide fuel for bush fires. There was I, the all-knowing, all-powerful white man, doing a task which was definitely anti-Life Force, and there was Joseph, the ignorant savage, knowing perfectly well – *feeling* perfectly well – that what I was doing was unworthy and wrong. And didn't he let me know he knew it too! I used to get the feeling that Joseph knew the white man was something that Africa had to put up with, for a time at least, but that he was a force for evil, and not a force for good. I used to *feel* that myself then – now I *know* it too.

Can we ask ourselves – what purpose of the Life Force did Joseph and his brethren fulfil? Would it have been better for the purposes of the Life Force if all of Mankind had remained at that stage of development?

Palaeolithic Man made so little impact on the rest of Nature that he didn't really change it at all, for better or for worse. He played a worthy part in the balance of Nature, but not a big part. It can be imagined (from our anthropomorphic point of view at least) that it was good that the teeming Life of this planet should come up with *self-awareness* – with a manifestation that could look and marvel and stand in wonder and in awe of the superb beauty of the world. What is the point, one might ask, of all that beauty with no beholder – with all that splendour and no one in awe? Joseph, the only Palaeolithic man I have ever known intimately, had an astonishing sensitivity to the Universe. He used to point out, constantly, the beauty and wonder of things to *me*. He saw far more than I did – saw deeper – felt more strongly. All his life he was 'high' though he never drank alcohol and took no drugs.

Is that enough reason for being? Is it not good that the Life Force, having developed the stars and the planets, and clothed one planet with green life of enormous complexity and beauty, should develop the capacity of Life to contemplate itself – to stand amazed at its own beauty? Is that not enough?

Again, I can ask the question. I cannot supply the answer.

CHAPTER TWO

Of Neolithic Man

*The Earth, gentle and indulgent, ever mindful of the needs of man,
spreads his walks with flowers, and his table with plenty; returns with
interest every good committed to her care, and though she produces the
poison, she provides the antidote.*
Pliny, *Natural History*, 1.ii

WHEN JOSEPH AND I were wandering in the veld and feeling
very thirsty, for the air in that country is like the breath of
a blast furnace, Joseph would notice a small straggly creeper
lying on the ground. With his spearhead he would dig down
into the ground beneath it and reveal a growth about the size
of a melon. This he would pull out, and we would take turns to
suck the juice out of it. It tasted horrible, but on one occasion it
may have saved our lives. I liked it less than the gallon of good
pure water, slightly acid and warm, of course, which we used to
find inside the paunch of any gemsbok we killed. I have drunk
many a cupped double handful of that. I can taste it now.

A thing that interested me more was what Joseph called
'Bushman wheat', because I felt then, and I feel now, that it was
this invention or discovery that led to the next change in
mankind's relationship with the rest of Nature.

18

There is a certain kind of ant which collects grass seeds in large quantities. These seeds are stored underground, and mould is allowed to grow on them (the ants actually inoculate the seed with the right mould) and the ants live on the mould. The ancestors of the Bushmen found that they could gather these seeds, crush them between two stones, roast them on a flat stone, and eat them. This is what Joseph called 'Bushman wheat'.

I am quite certain in my own mind, because it seems so completely obvious, that it was through ant-collected grass seeds that Man, or Woman, discovered agriculture. Of course sooner or later people would have observed that this grass seed, spilled on the ground in the rainy season, would sprout. In the right conditions it would have grown, set seed itself, and then died. To collect enough seed for a meal from the sparsely growing grasses of the bush-veld would have been a very unrewarding job, but when a pound or two of seed, already taken by the ants and then robbed from them by Man, was inadvertently left in a wet place such a thick mass of grass would grow up all in one place that harvesting of the crop of seed it produced would have been possible. Agriculture was thus born.

And then some time about twenty thousand years ago – the wink of an eye in the geological time-scale – wheat was evolved. This was an example of one of those apparently miraculous pieces of symbiotic development that makes the study of Life so infinitely fascinating. A certain grass produced offspring which had suffered a mutation, in other words which were 'freaks'. They had the wrong number of chromosomes. Left to itself this mutated form would quickly have died out, because the seeds were far too heavy to be blown by the wind and had no other device for distribution. Many grass seeds have arrangements for hooking on to animals (barley does), others have light seeds that can be windborne, other grains hang their heads far over away from

19

the parent plant (like oats) so that the seeds fall on new ground, or, helped by the wind, even further away. But this new species, wheat, had no way of spreading its seed around at all. Left to itself even the most primitive of wheat just drops its seeds all in a heap right by the stalk of the parent plant. And that's just no way to survive. Left to itself wheat – either our modern varieties or the most primitive varieties ever known – would just die out. (Maize is another plant that could not survive without Man.)

What saved wheat was Man. The new mutation came about just when Man had developed agriculture. For Man this was the perfect food grain. Easy to grow, easy to harvest, easy to thresh (the seed is naked), easy to mill, easy to bake and good to eat. And for wheat Man was the perfecting distributing agent. Has any plant ever evolved a better way of distributing its seed than to find an animal which will put the seeds at the right depth under cleared and manured ground, at just the right spacing, and then carefully protect and nurture the growing crop?

Wheat + Man = Civilisation.

And the plant, the animal and the concept spread slowly across the land surfaces of the planet. (In the monsoon countries of Asia rice fulfilled the same sort of purpose, in Central America maize, and in the Andes the potato).

The 'wild' Bushman divides his time between hunting, gorging, digesting and dancing. He sleeps while he is digesting. A party of Bushmen will kill a buck (generally by shooting it from very short range with a tiny poisoned arrow when it comes to drink), light a fire, and proceed to char rather than cook the offal, the meat, the stomach and guts, the bone marrow, and even sometimes the skin. They eat and eat until their bellies are distended like balloons. They sleep – and gorge – and sleep – and gorge. Then, the meat all gone, they get hungry and go hunting again. If there is no game nearby they simply pick up their few belongings and trek off into the veld looking for it. Verily these people have 'no fixed abode'.

With agriculture all was different. If you plant a crop you have got to protect it and, ultimately, harvest it. You have got to stay in the same place. This means building a hut, and ultimately a village. This makes possible the accumulation of possessions.

The Bushman woman carries a skin satchel and a gemsbok horn. The gemsbok has long straight horns, needle-sharp. A dog can be disembowelled by one of them. Every woman carries one of these to use as a digging-stick and it is perfect for its purpose. The skin satchel is for carrying back the food that she collects in the veld – *veldkos* it is called by white and black alike. *Veldkos* consists of bulbs or corms that are to be found underground in the bushveld. When meat is short the people eat *veldkos* – when there has been a kill they don't bother about it.

The Bushman carries his bow, a quiver of arrows on his back, often a skin satchel as well, a few bits and pieces and odds and ends, like a little pouch of arrow poison (one poison is made from a beetle, another from a plant), some charms and beads. Both men and women wear a string around their waists with pieces of skin hanging down fore and aft. It is the privilege of the old man of the family group to kindle a fire at each new campsite. He does this by rotating a stick with a bow-string, so that it bores into the side of a piece of wood. Fire results.

The true 'wild' Bushman never builds huts. He throws up a very crude shelter or wind-break and sleeps or crouches in the lee of that. I am quite certain that the reason why he does not build huts is not because he can't – it is because he doesn't want to. The true Bushman does not *want* possessions. He likes a knife, if he can get it. (When I call him Stone Age Man I ignore the fact that he does, in fact, carry on a very limited trade with Bantu or white men, for such things as knives and

21

iron spearheads, although very few Bushmen in fact carry spears. Joseph was an exception.) He needs the few items I have enumerated above, all of which he can very easily provide for himself from the bush in which he swims like a fish, and he just does not want anything else, except sometimes ostrich egg shells, which he uses to carry water. Sometimes a party of Bushmen will fill a number of ostrich shells with water (during the rainy season), seal the hole in them with tree-gum, and bury them. Then, if the group comes back to that place in the dry season, the members know there will be water there.

But how different is the case of the agriculturalist!

In the first place he *needs* possessions. No doubt the horns of antelope, or the antlers of deer in northern latitudes, served him as digging sticks until he learned to make better ones from fire-hardened wood. Then he learned to tip wood with stone. Then he needed a sickle, which he made from a piece of wood with sharp flints set in it.

As agriculture developed he needed more and more implements. From dragging bushes over the ground to smooth the clods he no doubt soon invented the harrow. There were fine Neolithic harrows made of wooden frames, and no doubt there still are, because somewhere in this world you can still find people at every stage of human development.

There were other possessions that Neolithic Man needed, and these were weapons of war. Not just tiny bows and arrows for shooting buck. (It is no good shooting poisoned arrows into enemies in a battle – for all these poisons take hours to work. Your enemy will have killed you long before he is dead.) Spears, shields, clubs (*kirries* in Southern Africa – *rungu* in East), and throwing-axes all became necessary. War had begun.

The reasons for this are fairly obvious. Firstly, mankind now had something worth stealing. No Bushman is going to steal the bow and arrows of another – it is just too easy for him to

22

make a bow and arrows for himself. There are, it is believed, small fights or squabbles between groups of Bushmen but they practically never lead to death.

The Bushmen practise a most effective form of birth control. The mothers not only suckle their babies for two or three years after birth, but carry them constantly and during this period there is a strong inhibition against sexual intercourse. The exigencies of the nomadic hunting life, too, probably make conception a fairly rare event. In any case, from what I saw myself of the way 'wild' Bushmen spend their nights – in almost constant dancing – they wouldn't have much time for anything else! So the only reason for warfare would have been when two family groups impinged on one another's territory, and this would seldom have happened because the population was so small. It probably *never* happened until the Neolithic or Bronze Age Bantu began to drive down from the North and take up the Bushman hunting grounds.

Come agriculture this rapidly changed.

Settled people, living in houses and with privacy, and well-fed, breed. They love to see the little children running about. The populations began to increase. Further, there was now something to steal. Crops were grown, and garnered, and stored. What a temptation these would be for starving people. Also, as more and more people took to this new settled way of life, one can imagine squabbles over the best agricultural land. There wasn't very much of it. It is a laborious job to cut down trees with stone axes and then remove the stumps. Naturally open ground, well drained, would have been in great demand. Wars began, and weapons became necessary.

The first agriculturalists did not, of course, abandon hunting altogether. They still went on with their old hunting and gathering exercises. The honey was still robbed from the wild bees. Farming enables people to gather in far larger units. Bushman groups seldom number more than a dozen, or a couple of dozen at most. The area of country that a group can hunt and collect over will not support greater numbers in one place. The mounting stores of grain made it possible for large communities to collect, and build large villages.

There was safety in numbers. When wars and raiding started, the bigger groups tended to win. Politics started. Discipline started. The community that obeyed its chief survived – the one that was too anarchic lost the battles. Tribal organisation grew up. People speaking the same language tended to ally themselves together, under one paramount chief. In this lay safety, and success in war. Most of the black peoples of Africa are at this stage of development now. The reason why the Western-style nation-state is so difficult to achieve in Africa is simply this. The Bantu people of Africa (and the Nilotics, Hamites, Semi-Hamites and all the rest of them) are tribesmen first and last and no tribesman is going to vote against his tribal brother in an election. Hence the government of an African nation-state is almost always the government of the majority tribe over the others. People deplore this and think it a terrible thing. 'The tribal barriers must be broken down,' they say. Of course they should not be broken down – they should be reinforced. They are the strongest and most positive thing in Africa. All tribal areas should be self-governing, with just enough of some federal structure to stop tribes from fighting one another too much. Political harmony would result.

But what of the purpose of this chapter – to examine the relationship between Neolithic Man and the rest of Nature?

Mankind extended enormously his knowledge of, and sympathy with, the rest of Nature by the discovery of agriculture. For he still remained a hunter, fisherman and collector, but he also became a husbandman. He suddenly found he could interfere with the rest of Nature for his own uses and survival.

Of course when a Bushman shoots a gemsbok he is interfering with the rest of Nature, but he is doing it in a very direct and casual manner. His activity has no noticeable ecological effect: the killing of one buck among thousands makes no difference to the ecological balance of the region. But once the digging-stick came in, and the felling axe – albeit a stone one – and fire, Mankind really began to be something rather special. He could actually alter the landscape. He could radically affect the balance of other species. He could increase in numbers himself until he was too numerous for the local biosphere easily to support. When this happened he had to modify the local biosphere even more – cut down more forest – clear more ground – eliminate more wild animals which ate his crops – destroy more weeds.

And then he domesticated animals. The 'wild' Bushmen of the Kalahari and Namib don't even have dogs. Joseph used to borrow three dogs from his Berg Damara neighbours to hold at bay the gemsbok that either he speared or I shot.

In Neolithic times Man really began to shape the landscape. The square fields whose traces we see on the chalk downs of southern England were made by Neolithic men. Because they had invented the plough, but not the mould-board which turns the earthen furrow, they needed to cross-plough. That is they needed to plough one way, with their pointed stick, and then plough again at right angles to it to break the soil properly and achieve a seed bed. Therefore they needed roughly square fields.

I believe this factor brought about a completely different way of looking at the Universe.

The Bantu of East, Central and Southern Africa, until the white man came, did not have the plough. Cultivation was done by women, generally after the men had felled and burned the standing timber that would have prevented it, with a hoe or digging-stick. Therefore it mattered not one jot to them what shape their fields were. I have seen thousands and

25

thousands of fields in Africa made by people who do not plough and I never saw a square field among them, remember seeing no straight lines – very few corners at all in fact – and certainly not one single right angle. The very concept of the straight-sided figure had not been thought of by these people.

The circle though was a different thing. The obvious shape for a grass and stick hut, or a mud and stick one, is round. Most of the Africans I met built the walls of their huts in a perfect circle – then built the framework of the roof on the ground – thatched it – and lifted the completed roof up and placed it on the walls. It was thus desirable that both walls and roofs should be perfect circles: thus they would be sure to fit each other. The Zulus in south-east Africa, and the Swazis too and a few other tribes, make splendid dome-shaped huts – there are no eaves to these – but even in their cases the huts are perfect circles. The circle is the natural shape for a thatched hut. Added to this these people make use of gourds for holding liquid. These are circular. Then they invented pottery and pots, again, are naturally circular. I have heard it said that Africans *think* in circles. Any Bantu African I have ever known can describe a circle immediately on the ground, or with a pencil on paper, and it will invariably be a perfect circle – much better than any I can describe. But ask him to delineate a *square* and – unless he has been to a missionary school – the result will be most peculiar

It may be objected that this is pretty irrelevant, and has nothing to do with the purpose of this chapter: to examine the relationship between Neolithic Man and the rest of Nature. I am not so sure. Straight lines are rare in Nature except when imposed by that natural phenomenon – Man. Right angles are practically non-existent. The earth is a globe – so are the heavenly bodies. I wonder if it is not possible that when Man began to think and feel in straight lines and right angles he made a big jump towards divorcing himself from the rest of

Nature – to thinking that he was not a part of Nature but something quite different?

The animal-drawn plough was a Neolithic invention though – a natural result of the domestication of animals – and the plough made necessary the straight line. You can plough in a curve – indeed the world would be a better place if more people did it, for contour ploughing would then more often be the rule and the erosion that is destroying our Earth would be prevented. But the obvious way to plough – and the best way on flat ground – is in straight lines. The straight line is thus a Neolithic invention. Then, if you use a scratch plough, as the Neolithic farmer did, and as millions of Indians and Egyptian cultivators do to this day, cross-ploughing becomes very desirable. The square field, what our archaeologists call the lynchet, becomes the rule. Man has invented the square. It has been forced upon him, in fact, by farming. It is not a far step from that to square or rectangular houses. Man is getting further all the time from Nature-not-Man.*

Now the effects of the Neolithic Revolution on Man's conception of the rest of Nature were profound. For one thing, religion was invented. Not the natural, animistic, religion of my friend Joseph and his fellows, who just felt that the whole Universe was divine and significant, and knew that there was some force or power that moved the whole of Nature, including them – but organised religions invented by priests. Priestcraft was invented. The new discipline that was made necessary by settled communities – and warring communities – could be immensely strengthened by priests.

Priests, who were freed from toil and therefore had time to think, and observe the stars and study other aspects of Nature, were in a very strong position to impose their wills on people who had time to do none of these things. By inventing myths, and holding out hopes of Heaven and threats of Hell, they could get people to do very much what they wanted them to do.

27

Of course there were chiefs also – and kings by extension – and these people as a general rule managed to exert control over the priests. Sometimes they did it by combining the two roles: they were priest-kings. But if they were not they could generally keep the upper hand, as King Henry II proved when he sent the four knights to kill Thomas à Becket. It paid the priests to obey the kings – and it paid the latter to look after the priests. Together they made an invincible combination and could rule the people completely. The priests took the local tutelary deities that inhabited groves and mountains and lakes and streams in the minds of Palaeolithic people, and turned them into powerful and dangerous superhuman beings, to be feared and propitiated. The way to propitiate them was almost always to give goods or money to the priests. I have lined up in several Hindu temples, clutching a coconut that I have bought with good money (from the priests) in order to offer it ostensibly to the God but actually to the priests, for it to be broken by the priests, and its water poured into a vessel to be consumed by the priests, as also its flesh. The priests would not have bought the coconut from the cultivator in the first place of course. It would have been given as a free offering.

Undoubtedly the priest-king combination made a powerful force, and it has been very seldom in human history that any commoners have been able to break away from it.

Of course the people *needed* authority – they *needed* discipline. How else could they avoid squabbling over their fields – how else repulse enemies?

And then, also in the Neolithic period, came the development that led more quickly than anything else to the centralised state: irrigation.

In the northern jungle of Sri Lanka there are *kulams* everywhere. These are small tanks as local white people call them – not tanks at all but small earth dams that impound a certain amount of water. This water is used for irrigating fields to make food-growing possible in this very dry forest.

True there are cultivators in that northern jungle who farm without irrigation – by a slash-and-burn cultivation, locally called *chena*. The British, when they ruled the island, set their faces against this with dire results: thousands of people starved because they were not allowed to farm in the only way they could. There was no 'dole' in those days. In fact *chena* cultivation is not harmful to the rest of Nature at all, provided that the population does not get out of balance: the fields cleared from the jungle, and abandoned after a few years (not because the nutrients are exhausted but because arable weeds take over) soon revert to jungle again and provided the cultivators do not come back too soon (thirty years is about the minimum acceptable period) no harm is done to the *soil* whatever. And it is the *soil* that is important to the Life Force – on the soil all terrestrial life depends. I am talking about the dry *chena* jungle of northern Sri Lanka here – not the rain forests of Amazonia.

But irrigation is another kettle of fish altogether. People make the little *kulams* or small earthern dams, which store enough water for a family or a village, and they build a family home near them, or a village indeed, and live, perforce, very settled lives. Having put in all that expenditure of energy they cannot just move on. They have to maintain the fertility of the soil downhill from the *kulams,* which they can irrigate, and therefore they learn to practise a very sound, enduring, and organic agriculture.

Further, in the village-sized *kulam* settlement, there must be a very stable village community. Communal effort is needed to maintain the *kulam,* communal effort to distribute the water, communal effort to share it out equitably. A strong village community results, and it may be that this is the most pleasing arrangement of human beings for our putative Life Force. It can certainly be beautiful to live in. Further, the *kulam* type community is almost independent of the rest of the world. It may do a very limited trade with it (it will almost certainly get raided by the tax-collectors of the central government and have part of its produce taken away) but it doesn't *need* a central government, and it doesn't *need* to co-operate much with other village communities. All it really wants is to leave other people alone and be left alone.

But along came another development, still in Neolithic times: the large-scale irrigation scheme. There are some fine examples of this in Sri Lanka, both ancient and modern.

In the Andes before the Europeans arrived, the people never invented bronze or iron: they never got out of the New Stone Age or Neolithic period. They developed, though, the most extensive and elaborate and sophisticated irrigation systems that have ever been on this planet.

Here was an opportunity for the priests, and the kings, and the priest-kings! Strong, large-scale, highly centralised organisation was absolutely necessary! Without it who would maintain the hundreds of miles of canal walls – the dams – the weirs – the sluices and all the rest of it? Why, the cultivator was absolutely dependent, in many cases, on engineering works being maintained hundreds of miles away from where he lived! He *had* to obey the priests and the kings.

The latter, of course, became enormously powerful. They could indulge their every whim. The choicest of young girls were theirs for the taking. Unfortunately a man's sexual appetites are pretty limited, even a king's and so just the ordinary business did not satisfy them and they had to indulge in such fancies as tearing the palpitating hearts out of living maidens with obsidian knives.

They built great cities. Cities are an inevitable result of large-scale irrigation. Babylon has become the symbol of them all. 'By the waters of Babylon I sat down and wept!' Undreamed-of luxury became possible. Tremendous differences arose between rich and poor. There was one thing that became normal in all large-scale-irrigation civilisations – the people of the cities relieved the cultivator of everything that he could grow except *just* enough to keep him alive. They still do of course.

In the great river valleys of China, in the Ganges and Indus and Godavari basins, in Mesopotamia, the lower Nile Valley, in the Andes and in Mexico, these great, gaudy, completely despotic, priest-ridden and king-oppressed civilisations developed and survived. Never perhaps, up to that time at least, had men and women distanced themselves so far from the rest of living Nature. As far as the dweller in Babylon, or Mohenjo-daro, was concerned Nature might not have existed at all. There were the peasants out on the irrigated acres, all of which were *owned* by the city dwellers, growing food for the benefit of those city dwellers, but the city dwellers themselves would not have known how to grow a thing. They never saw a tree, in those sun-baked mud-brick streets. They never went outside the walls, unless they had to. Inside they had every luxury that mankind knew about. There were plenty of poor people inside the city to wait upon them of course – slaves aplenty. It was always easy for the king to recruit the young peasants into his armies: for them it was relief from drudgery, and with them he could oppress the other peasants.

But the people of these large-scale-irrigation cities were even more divorced from the rest of Nature than are the inhabitants of Pittsburgh, or London, or Birmingham, or Tokyo, today. They scarcely had to know that it existed.

And I have seen, in Baghdad, Kerman, Yezd, Zahidan, Hyderabad, the old city of Delhi and a dozen other ancient Indian cities, people living like this by the hundred. People who would only leave the walls of their city if they absolutely had to, and then would look upon it as a penance.

I spent a week in the cellar of a rich landowner in Yezd, which is a city in the southern part of the great Persian desert. Why the cellar? – because in that violent heat the cellar, which was surmounted by a huge brick ventilator which looked southwards to catch what little wind there was that blew from the Indian Ocean, was the only place where it was possible to live without the most acute discomfort.

All the time I was there the merchant/landowner was visited by people from outside, who addressed him very deferentially, and gave him to read scrolls, and documents, and other bits of parchment and paper, all written in Farsi and embellished by many seals. He read them, signed some, sent others off again, had words with the messengers, wrote out Farsi cheques and other money-conveyances, and I asked him what all this was about.

'It's about *land*,' he said (through his eldest son who was educated in Tehran and spoke French). 'And *crops*. And *rents*.'

'Do you own much land?' I asked.

'Many acres. Many villages.'

'Are you a farmer yourself?' I asked.

'Know nothing about it. Have never touched a plough.'

'Do you go and *see* your land?' I asked.

'Never. There is no need for me to see it,' he said. 'The rents are collected. I never go further than the walls of Yezd.'

I felt I was talking to a member of a class that had endured right through the ages since men first dug a canal to bring water for the thirsty desert.

I do not claim, of course, that my landowner was a Neolithic man. He was anything but. His period was, of course, pure medieval. He was as Medieval as Chaucer's merchant. I merely mention him to show how far divorced from non-human Nature the inhabitants of the great irrigation cities could get. My Persian host was a Muslim of course, and believed strongly in one God, and spent much of his time praying to Him or reading the Koran or thinking about religion. His God was about as far as a God could get from the Great Spirit of Joseph the Bushman: so far from Nature that his worshippers were actually forbidden to depict any natural thing in His temples – abstract geometrical designs were all that were permitted.

Also, I am not implying that the large-scale-irrigation civilisations were in any way typical of the Neolithic period. The Neolithic people who came to Pembrokeshire, where I lived when I wrote this, and built the splendid *cromlech,* or 'chamber tomb', right near me, were in no way city people. They were herdsmen and cultivators, lived in scattered settlements of round huts, hunted game when they could, went down to the sea or the rivers and caught fish, were probably deeply religious, lived very close to the rest of Nature, and certainly had no feeling that Nature was anything they were not completely part of themselves.

Their attitude to the rest of Nature is typically expressed by Black Elk, a priest of the Sioux Nation of North Americans, as quoted in *Black Elk Speaks* recorded by John Neihardt:

> It is the story of all life that is holy and is good to tell, and of we two-leggeds sharing it with the four-leggeds and the wings of the air, and all green things: for these are children of one mother and their father is one Spirit.

But somewhere, probably in central Europe down towards the eastern Alps, men were discovering that, if you heated certain rocks, molten metals could be made to run from them, and these metals would cool, and solidify, and could be beaten into different shapes.

First bronze, and then iron, and after that steel, ushered in a whole new ball-game as regards Mankind's assessment of his part in, or outside of, the rest of Nature, which is what this book is about.

---

* It is interesting to consider here – although it has possibly no bearing at all on our subject – that Technological Man is going back, in some instances, to the circular field. In Libya and other flat desert areas, bore-holes are being sunk for water, and the water is being sprinkled on to the land by huge revolving spray arms. These thus

describe perfect circles. Ploughing and other cultivation is done spirally, which is quite convenient, and the result of such cultivation is a pattern of circles, just touching each other at their perimeters, with roughly triangular shapes of un-irrigated and uncultivated ground in between. I have often thought that a good way to bring under cultivation a large flat plain, whether originally wooded or not, would be to describe perfectly circular fields, and then leave, or else plant trees in, the small areas left between the circles. The homesteads could be situated in smaller circles in the middle of the fields. All cultivation could be done spirally, which saves turning at headlands. But Western man is so used now to thinking in straight lines and rectangles that such a course is very unlikely to be tried out.

CHAPTER THREE

Of Bronze Age and Iron Age Man

The teeming summer has come, bringing life in its arms, and strews rosy flowers on the face of hill and dale. In lovely harmony the wood has put on its green mantle, and summer is on her throne, playing her music. The willow whose harp hung silently when it was withered in winter, now gives forth melody. Hush – listen – the world is alive. The God Lugh stretches his long white arm above the hills. Across the sky fly the immortal children of light, the white Swans of Lir. They call upon their sister who gilds their wings with gold.
Bronze Age Irish Poem.

They make a desert and call it peace.
Pictish Chief referring to the Romans.

THE HOMERIC GREEKS WERE Bronze Age people and their attitude towards the rest of nature is indicated very well by their Gods. These were simply anthropomorphosed symbols of the various forces of Nature. The very fact that the Greeks turned these forces into *people* showed that they believed that people were part of Nature. There is no hint here that anybody thought, in those times, that Mankind was apart from Nature or Nature anything but the same stuff and substance that Mankind was made of. Poseidon was not only the Spirit of the Sea – he was a Man. And a God.

35

In Hindu India, particularly in the south of the subcontinent, I have often felt, or imagined I have felt, the spirit of the Bronze Age. Here we have, still existing and all-alive-o today, a system of Gods very similar to the ones the Greeks had. Nature absolutely bubbles over in the art of Hindu temples, Man (and especially Woman) take their full part in it, and the Animal-Gods are as important as the People-Gods. Hanuman the Monkey-God, Nagra the Cobra-God, Ganesh the Elephant-God are accorded full importance. Man and Nature are still one, and this is just as true today as it was four thousand years ago when some of the Hindu epics were written down.

It might here be opportune to discuss the attitude of present-day Hindus to the rest of Nature. It is one of complete acceptance that Mankind is a part of Nature, no more important than any other part, but also of complete *passivity* towards the rest of Nature. All organisms are working out their *Karma,* and all you have to do is leave them alone.

Ideally (but not practically) no Hindu will kill any animal for any reason whatever. Typical of this attitude is the tolerance towards cows and bullocks that wander the streets of all Indian cities at will, pinch vegetables from vendors' stalls, lick out the contents of the beggar's bowl while the owner is asleep. Typical too is the *ryot*, or farmer, who knows that his children do not have enough to eat, who will chase the monkeys from his crops by shouts but never dream of taking a gun out and shooting one – the only method that could possibly be effective at driving them away for any length of time whatever. Typical is the owner of an unwanted bull-calf who turns it loose (because the owner needs the milk of the mother) knowing full well it will die, but will not kill it or eat it because this would be taking life.

My own belief is that the Hindu inhibition about killing things is an aberration and not at all what the Life Force really requires. For the lands over which such abstinence is practised become hideously overgrazed by starving cattle and inevitably erode, thus coming eventually to support very little Life at all. Monkeys and wild pigs ravage the sparse crops, the trees are destroyed so there is no firewood for the people and they must burn dung – the dung that is desperately needed to put back into the starving soil.

I have lived in Hindu villages, and travelled through hundreds of them, and I have been convinced that the intention of the Life Force is *not* that Man should abstain from interfering with Nature at all. Much of Hindu India is going down a one-way road of soil exhaustion, impoverishment and ultimately starvation, simply because the people, although they will interfere with the vegetable kingdom to a fault, will not control the numbers of the animal kingdom. The carnivores have been eliminated all right (you could travel all your life in the populated parts of India and never see or hear – or hear of – a tiger) and there is nothing to control the herbivores and omnivores save Man, who stays his hand and thus fails to play his proper part in the balance of Nature.

But there is nowhere in Hindu belief or philosophy the idea that Man is in any way apart from Nature – particularly the animal part of it. The belief in reincarnation, which is central to it, supposes incarnation in innumerable animal forms besides human ones. The general idea is that the most primitive animals die, their souls reincarnate into higher forms of animal life, and so on, throughout the aeons of time, until they reach the stage of Mankind. In Man the soul achieves free will and can act badly or well. If badly – then the next reincarnation will be well down the scale again. If well, it will be into a superior man or woman. It is like a game of snakes and ladders. The ultimate goal is *perfection*. The soul is reincarnated into a very high quality human, and there are millions of reincarnations in each one of which it manages to strive a little higher towards perfection. Then after a final lifetime of striving to free the soul from the flesh, Nirvana is reached (according to the Buddhists), or the complete loss of individual identity, and the union of the soul with God – 'as a drop of water ultimately rejoins the Ocean'.

So although the Hindu totally accepts that he is part of Nature, he considers Nature too, like all matter, really an irrelevance and an illusion.

The Hindu system of thought has come up with marvellous insights and enlightenments over the last five or six hundred years. The Hindu ideal of 'non-attachment' is a necessary and essential step towards the sort of enlightenment that hopefully may one day resolve the problems of attaining our true place in Nature and of realising our true purpose. But my own feeling is that the Hindu is too preoccupied with his own personal salvation, or enlightenment, or perfection, to be able to play the active and positive part in the Dance of Nature intended by creation.

The Hindu *ryot* ploughs and sows and reaps infertile ground, because he *has* to. The people who parasitise him dream and meditate and strive for personal perfection, and the land gets more and more *unlike* the Garden of Eden.

As iron replaced bronze, Man became enormously powerful. The iron axe enabled him to clear-fell the forests and cultivate land never ploughed before. The iron ploughshare enabled him to plough it effectively, and cultivate the heavy land of the valley bottoms previously denied to the farmer. The iron-tipped arrow and spearhead made Man supreme over all the brutes. It was probably at this stage that people began to feel that Man had a divine right to clear and use for his own purposes any part of the world he wished, and destroy any living creature.

And then came steel, and the Romans, and steel gave them an enormous advantage over other men who hadn't got it. The Romans conquered the 'known' world. We Europeans tend to ignore all history except that of Europe, but probably equivalent things were happening in other places. We know great empires were established in India, and some of them were marvellously civilised and benign ones, before the Islamic invasions all but drove Hindu culture underground. But the Roman Empire can serve as an example of it all.

At first the Romans worshipped the old Gods of the elements, as the Greeks had done, and no doubt the hardy Italian cultivators had a very healthy relationship with the rest of Nature as well. But the steel-clad armies marched outwards, and conquered wherever they went, slaves poured into Rome, and rich Romans achieved a luxury probably never before or since achieved on this Earth. Machines nowadays make for luxury, washing machines save work, the teamaker wakes us with a gentle bell and hot tea, but *nothing* can be so luxurious as having lots and lots of obedient slaves.

In some ways it almost seems as if the Roman attitude towards Nature was an aberration – a flash in the pan.

Nothing like it had occurred before and for nearly two thousand years nothing like it occurred again. Of course there were civilised Romans, and stages of the history of Rome were civilised indeed. Some Roman poets wrote beautifully about Nature and the husbandry of the soil (notably Virgil), and many noble Romans no doubt lived at peace among their olive trees and grapevines, tended by contented slaves with a due respect for Mother Earth.

But the system of agriculture that gradually grew up in Italy (to which our own large-scale agribusiness bears such an astonishing resemblance) was the system of *latifundia*, the huge slave-worked estates. The displaced peasants could swarm into Rome and live on a dole of free bread.

The master lived far away in Rome too, and left the 'farming' to overseers. There is nobody as good as your jumped-up pleb for using a whip. The land was farmed on a purely extractive basis – for *profit*. It was not farmed to feed the people on it, or if it was, that was incidental. It was farmed to produce as big a money profit as possible for the aristocratic owner back in Rome, competing with other big estate owners to find more and more extravagant ways of spending it.

Unlike in our own day there were no artificial chemicals – no selective weed-killers, no machines, only the sweat of slaves. The crops, consumed in Rome, ended up as sewage going down the Tiber into the sea. The land lost its heart and became barren and infertile and it took many centuries before it would grow good crops again.

Virgil, in his *Eclogues*, movingly describes the sadness of a Roman peasant displaced by the new regime.

But the rest of us must go from here and be dispersed –
To Scythia, bone-dry Africa, the chalky spate of Oxus,
Even to Britain – that place cut off at the very world's end.
And, when shall I see my native land again? After long years,
Or never? – see the turf-dressed roof of my simple cottage,
And wondering gaze at the ears of corn that were all my kingdom.
To think of some godless soldier owning my well-farmed fallow.
A foreigner reaping these crops! To such a pass has civil
Dissension brought us . . .
No more singing for me.

And:

Oh, Lycidas, that I should have lived to see an outsider
Take over my little farm – a thing I had never feared.
And tell me, 'You're dispossessed, you old tenants, you've got to go.'
We're down and out. And look how Chance turns the tables on us.
These are *his* goats (rot them) you see me taking to market.

(translated by C. Day Lewis)

40

All this sadness to make way for the new *latifundia* – the huge slave-worked agribusinesses, the soul purpose of which was to make rich men richer, provide bread for city parasites and ruin the soil. How very close is the comparison with the chemical-worked agribusinesses of our own day.

Not to worry – there was North Africa. The remains of huge grain stores there indicate the scale of wheat production in areas which have now reverted to barren desert. The Italian landlords ceased to bother to farm their estates at all – towards the end of the Roman Empire nearly all the wheat for the *panem* part of *panem et circenses* came from Africa. It is impossible not to draw parallels with the present day.

And what became the Roman attitude towards the rest of Nature? Well their attitude towards animals was simple: slaughter them in vast numbers, and in the most curious ways, in the arena to amuse the people of Rome or the other provincial cities. North Africa was practically denuded of large wild animal life by the insatiable appetite of the arenas. Wild animals and human dissidents died in countless thousands in the arenas of the Roman Empire.

I have walked into the ruins of Greek theatres and felt my spirit soar as I breathed the atmosphere of freedom and wit and intellect and fun and justice towards all creatures. I have walked into a Roman amphitheatre and shuddered with horror as the atmosphere of slaughter and sadism and mindless brutality has almost overwhelmed me. *Ugh!*

But thank whatever Tendency there be, the Barbarian came down like a cleansing fire and swept it all away and the spirit of man could breathe free again. *One* experiment was over.

During the Iron Age war became very common among humans and although this fact is deplored by most people the fact that it is so deplored is a measure of the importance that Man places on the welfare of Man, and the lack of importance that he places on the rest of Nature.

The wars between humans would have been *welcomed* by the rest of Nature, if the rest of Nature was conscious and could welcome anything, for they kept Man's numbers down. They kept Mankind in reasonable proportion. They kept him from getting out of hand. Maybe they were a device of the Life Force to do just this. Has anybody ever thought of that before? Plagues came too, and served the same purpose, and so did the occasional friendly famine. Mankind's numbers were kept well within reason right through the Dark Ages to Medieval times, and when, in the fourteenth century, the species looked like getting out of hand along came the good old Black Death.

The attitude of Man to the rest of Nature during the Iron Age, if we exclude Imperial Rome, was casual, tolerant, and robust. All through the world there were sacred groves, sacred streams, sacred springs, sacred oaks. Nymphs and fawns peopled the woods in men's imaginations. Pagan Man did not feel himself estranged from the rest of Nature: he must have felt himself very much a part of it, albeit a dominant part. After the collapse of the Roman Empire he certainly did not have a feeling of arrogance or overwhelming superiority. Mankind did not weigh heavily on the rest of life. Britain, as an example, remained substantially covered with woods. The cultivated areas were just clearings in the forest.

I have lived with Iron Age people in several parts of Africa. Wars between tribes were at a standstill when I was there because we had the *Pax Britannica* – if tribesmen fought the British knocked their heads together. But before the Zulu Wars the great Zulu nation, which consisted not of members of one tribe but an amalgam of tribespeople mostly conquered by Chaka, the original 'Black Napoleon', swept through south-eastern Africa, and conquered and slaughtered, and conquered and slaughtered – and kept the population down very well indeed. What would have happened had the white man not intervened is anybody's guess – certainly the Zulu conquests seem to have been something new in Africa.

An off-shoot of the Zulu hordes crossed the Limpopo to form the Ndebele nation in what is now called Zimbabwe, and which quickly enslaved the resident Shona. Another off-shoot crossed the Zambezi into north-eastern Zambia and became the all-conquering Angoni, and yet another, further west, founded the Barotse nation, which is still strong and pretty independent today. I spent two years of my life travelling their country inoculating their cattle to wipe out contagious bovine pleuro-pneumonia – with success I might add.

The Balozi, as the Barotseland ruling race were called then (I don't know what they are called now – most names have been changed since the whites left) were a typical Iron Age people. Their heartland was the huge floodplain of the upper Zambezi, three hundred miles wide – a dead flat plain, grassed all over, flooded every year for three months after the rains to the depth of a foot or two but dry the rest of the year.

The Balozi cultivated maize and other crops, but their principal wealth was cattle. The great herds of cattle were driven off to the higher unflooded ground (all forested) when the plain was flooded. The move to the uplands was officially opened by King Yeta II, who made a marvellous ceremonial exit from the flooded plains in his magnificent state barge. The villages of the plain were all on slightly raised ground and a few old people stayed in them during the floods – the rest all went off with the cattle.

The district I worked in was Sesheke District, further down the river and not contiguous with the great flood plain, although I traversed the plain twice by barge propelled by eighteen paddlers. The paddlers stood up, fore and aft, and punted in the shallow water. The tops of the grasses showed well above the surface of the water so it looked as if we were navigating in an endless grassy plain. The bow of the flat-bottomed barge parted the grass as she proceeded – and left a wake of clear water astern. We camped each night either on the raised hump of a village, or on a termite hill. But in my district the people did not have to migrate annually, but lived by 'slash and burn'. The ceremonial symbol of the men was an ornamental axe, that of the women a hoe. For the men moved into a new area of forest and axed down the trees and burnt them. The women followed and hoed the ground and planted crops. After four or five years the land was exhausted (and foul with the weeds of arable land which had moved in) and the villagers moved on to another area.

As in Sri Lanka the effect of this agriculture on the rest of Nature was not as bad as it sounds. After the cultivators left, the forest would regenerate itself very quickly and provided the tree-fellers did not come back too soon, the soil would have been built up again to its fullest potential. Iron Age men did not bear too heavily on the rest of Nature at all. I believe though that a more permanent sustainable husbandry would have been more in accordance with the purposes of the Life Force.

As regards fellow animals – the land was full of big game. I could go out any evening I wanted to and shoot a buck and would seldom have to walk more than half a mile from my camp to do it. The reason for the abundance of game was that Iron Age Man did not have rifles. The British did not allow the 'Natives' to own firearms (except in very rare cases in which an exception had been made for chiefs). The natives (I use this word not in a derogatory sense but simply to mean 'the people indigenous to the country') hunted, with snares, pitfalls, and spears, but they did not succeed in killing many wild animals in that thick forest country. They depended for milk and meat on their cattle – game was an extra. The Bashikulumbwe people further north, in what we called the Hook of the Kafue Country, they did hunt much more seriously, but they were purely cattle and hunting people, with practically no cultivation of the soil. Their land was a vast grassy alluvial plain. They represented another, perhaps earlier, stage of the Iron Age. They built long fences of thornbush, funnel-shaped, and

44

drove the wild animals into it and slaughtered them with spears when they reached the apex. They used to hunt buffalo like this. They were famous for their hunting of lions. A ring of warriors would surround a lion – and close in chanting and shouting war cries. When the ring got small enough the lion would try to break out. It would charge one warrior. The latter would take the charge on his shield – and in seconds the lion would resemble a pin-cushion as a score of spears were flung into it. But the warrior that it had charged was generally dead.

But even this dedicated hunting never really reduced the numbers of wild beasts. The Kafue plain was teeming with buck and buffalo. Since the whites have left, however, any native who can afford one can own a rifle and I am told that in the Kafue plain big game is practically extinct. For non-human mammals in Africa it is the end of the road. If the present trend continues, within a decade or two there will be none of them left at all. Even the big game parks are swarming with poachers with rifles, and nobody can stop them. Is this what the Life Force intended? I very much doubt it.

Going back to the slash-and-burn agriculture (the bane of British forestry officers – they used to lie abed moaning about it) it was not a bad method of husbandry *provided the population kept small*. And it did keep small. One used to hear of various birth control measures. The simple expedient of husbands not sleeping with their wives while they were suckling was one of them. There was a strong inhibition against this and a woman would suckle a child for three years. Internecine war may have kept numbers down before the British came – but I doubt if many people were killed in such small wars, which were partly ritualistic. Child mortality was fairly high. Disease among adults was not a potent limiting factor – there was very little disease and most of the people I saw were radiant with health. But certainly, in those days before the Second World War, most of Central Africa was *not* overpopulated. I never came to a village and found people hungry, or with anything less than plenty to eat, and when I began to read about famines in Africa after the War, I could scarcely believe the reports. But during the last forty years the Iron Age culture has been destroyed, wiped out by the mad rush to enter the Brave New World, and famine stalks the savannah and the bush.

CHAPTER FOUR

Of Dark Age and Medieval Man

The harp music, and the clear voice of the poet, singing how Man was made long ago, and how God made the world a bright sea-enriched plain, made the sun and moon to light its inhabitants, clothed the earth with leaves and branches, gave life to all moving things.
From *Beowulf.*

THE NATURE GODS PREVAILED right through the Dark Ages, holding out century after century against the inroads of Christianity. Under their influence Mankind did little harm to the rest of Nature – had little effect on it. The Vikings roamed the seas, and left little behind them except their wakes. The English came to Albion and drove out, or intermarried with, the Welsh. The Welsh who were driven west then lived a pastoral life in their hills as some still do; while the English slowly, with the steel axe and the iron-shod plough, cut back the forests and replaced them with a permanent sustainable agriculture, but their fields remained clearings among the forest. In the forest they hunted and herded their pigs. The Gods that Man worshipped were, like the Greek Gods, and the Hindu Gods of today, idealised manifestations of Nature in human form. Man still felt himself part of Nature although an increasingly dominant part.

It is a strange fact, little understood in the more 'advanced' sectors of the Western world today, that you cannot *hunt* an animal without developing a sympathy for it. I have been a hunter all my life and have experienced, again and again, this great sympathy for the hunted. The men of the Dark Ages were hunters, and they could not have been successful hunters had they not developed this sympathy for the beasts they hunted.

The people of the Dark Ages almost certainly had this feeling for all wild nature. Their hunting of other animals was partly religious, partly ritualistic. *'Hob y deri dan do!'* ('The boar of the oakwoods is under the roof-tree!') sang the Welshmen after they had carried out a successful hunt, and similar songs, and rituals, and rejoicings, and incantations, were used by all hunters the world over and, in a few places, still are. This sort of thing has nothing to do with senseless slaughter, any more than has the little poisoned arrow of the Bushman. It is just Man playing his proper part in the rest of Nature and playing it with love and respect for the creatures hunted.

But, in Europe, Christianity had to prevail. Unlike the religions that came earlier, Christianity at first was very concerned with Man – hardly with the rest of Nature at all. Man, and his soul and its destination, were the real preoccupations. There was no feeling, as there is in Hinduism and by extension Buddhism, and as there was in probably all of the pre-Judaistic religions, that Man sprang from other animals and is one with them. Man was created separately (and Woman taken from his spare rib) and Man was given dominion over the beasts of the field and the birds of the air – and that was that.

It is quite easy to draw the conclusion, from both the Old and the New Testaments, that the Universe was created for the use and pleasure of Mankind. The Old Testament, and the Torah, do, in fact, inculcate a respect for the rest of Nature, but it is not the respect of participants but of masters. I am told by

Muslims, and people who have made a study of Islam, that Islam enjoins the same sort of respect, but I have read the Koran in translation, and come across very few such enjoinders.

Art is always a tell-tale indication of what is inside a culture, and Christian art has always had Man (and happily also Woman) in the centre of the picture and the rest of Nature, if it appears at all, as very much a background to the human story. Islamic art of course allows no depiction of Nature at all: it is purely abstract or mathematical art. But Islam is the faith of the deserts, where Nature hardly exists, and life is hard for Man, plant and beast. Whenever Islam has reached lusher, rainier regions it has lost its severe austerity, taken on local animistic beliefs, and become much more in tune with the world of Nature around it. The Moguls, once they got to India, even allowed themselves to depict the human form, most beautifully and sensuously, and to depict plants and animals too, in great profusion. The Prophet must have turned in his sandy grave.

The very first Christians – the Christians of the catacombs and the desert hermitages – were probably so preoccupied with their own salvation that they had very little time to think of the rest of Nature at all. Presumably they were brought face to face with it with a jolt when the lions were let out into the arenas. There is, of course, the lovely story of Androcles and the Lion, and there are many stories of early Christian saints and hermits living at peace with, and in sympathy with, the rest of Nature: St. Hubert and his deer, St. Paul the Hermit and his wild animals; and I cannot look out of my window here as I am writing this book without seeing the summit of Carn Ingli, on which little mountain St. Brynach, in the seventh century, used to meditate. St. Brynach had a stag which he used to use as a saddle horse and a wolf which herded his cattle for him, and he was guided to the place where he built his church (just down the road from where I live) by a white sow with five piglets. His empathy with other animals was complete.

And there is the story of Cuthbert, another Celtic saint, who, when he lived on the Farne islands of Northumberland, practising austerity, used to pray standing up to the neck in the sea. A brother monk relates of him:

> Thus did Cuthbert, as his wont was, sing his prayers standing in the sea-flood up to his neck, and, after, bowed his knees on the sand, stretching the palms of his hands to the heavenly sky. Just then came two otters from the bottom of the sea, and they with their fleeces dried his feet, and with their breath warmed his limbs, and, after, with beckonings, begged his blessings, lying at his feet in the yellow sand.

A medieval abbot would have sent for the otter hounds.

Celtic Christianity was, alas, driven away by the Roman variety, and in the Roman communion this great fellow-feeling with the rest of Nature was not so strong. Sexism came in too, in full swing. The Celtic Church admitted women priests, most monks and nuns were married, and many of the great abbeys were ruled by women. Only during the last two decades of our century has the unquestioned domination of the male in the Christian Church been challenged again; and it is still conducting a very fighting retreat.

There was a chance that Christianity could have taken a much more pro-Life turn right at its inception. According to the Essene Gospel Jesus, after having given his followers the Lord's prayer, said this: 'After this manner, pray to your Earthly Mother:

> Our Mother which art upon Earth, hallowed be thy name. Thy kingdom come and thy will be done in us as in thee. Thou sendest every day thy angels, send them to us also. Forgive us our sins as we atone all our sins against thee. And lead us not into sickness, but deliver us from all evil, for thine is the Earth, the body, and the wellbeing. Amen.'

There are three possibilities about the Essene Gospel, either it is a forgery of our own time and that seems unlikely, or it was simply invented by somebody who was a contemporary of Jesus, or Jesus actually said the things recorded in it but they were later suppressed. In any case it seems that the world was due for a massive swing towards belief in a solely masculine God at the time, and towards belief that the Universe was indeed created simply for the benefit of Mankind. Judaism had held this view for centuries and Islam, when it followed eventually, was completely male-centred. The obsession of the early Christian saints with personal salvation also implied turning their backs upon Nature-not-Man, although some of them did manage to find God through Nature – 'the living garment of God'. St. Francis of Assisi (recently appointed 'patron saint of ecology') and other early Christians could not get away from Nature-not-Man. And peasants and other common country people were always having to be corrected by the Fathers of the Church for the heresy of Mariolatry. They could not really believe that, although it was quite obvious that all Life came from the female (fertilised by the male of course), God should be exclusively male.

And with the development of the great monastic houses a new attitude to Nature began to appear. Man began to *interfere* with Nature to a new tune but, even so, very benignly. To me this interference represented a determined attempt by Mankind to exercise his proper function in the world.

The monks must have dwelt long upon the story of the Garden of Eden, and made it their business to try to recreate such a garden on Earth. The monks planted vines and fruit orchards, flower and herb gardens, they raised great flocks of sheep which grazed the pastures around their granges, they cleared some of the forest and used the timber for their great buildings – buildings that they put up for the glory of God – they ploughed the cleared land and planted and grew good crops of wheat. They increased greatly the fertility and

51

fruitfulness of the land. It is not a coincidence that Mendel was a monk.

It can be postulated that this planet was not 'meant', by the Life Force, to remain for ever jungle, forest, savannah and desert, but that intelligence was developed on it to increase its beauty and fertility and by ordering, increase the beauty and effectiveness of the living component; to augment Life and embellish the Earth.

Certainly all the signs that have come down to us from the great age of the monasteries indicate that these people lived in harmony with the rest of Nature and that, whatever their scriptures told them, the monks and nuns looked upon themselves as a part of Nature too. Their very buildings drew their inspiration straight from Nature: the pointed arch and vault, which took over from the practical and military romanesque, were taken straight from the arches and vaults of the trees in the forest; the piers and columns were embellished with foliar designs, and carvings of small animals appear everywhere.

Probably Man has never had a more positive and benign relationship with the rest of Nature than he had in the great period of the Cistercian monasteries. It was not just a *laissez-faire* relationship such as Stone Age Man enjoyed. The monks intervened in Nature, benignly and constructively. Whether many of us now would *wish* to get up at two o'clock every morning and get down on our knees on a cold stone floor, and either pray or work until nightfall, and never see a woman (or a man if you happened to be a woman) and never know the joy of playing with children, I very much doubt. I know the answer in my own case without a great deal of soul-searching or thought. And yet I remember the lake-island in Sri Lanka with the three wise gentle Buddhist monks on it and still sometimes wonder if I should not be there.

As for the secular world in the Middle Ages, mankind was divided into two almost separate species: the gentry and the hoi-polloi. The latter – serfs, cottars, villeins etc., were forced to have a benign relationship with the rest of Nature whether they wanted to or not. With simple tools they could do little harm. Slowly they pushed back the woods, and their herds of swine collected the acorns in the woods that were left, and fertilised the trees with their dung, and the peasants farmed carefully and well the land they had cleared. Their vision of themselves and their own role in Nature was quite clear, and stemmed, no doubt, from the story of Eden and the rest of the Old Testament. *The Vision of Piers Ploughman* makes their attitude obvious. They expected – and wanted – to toil and till the soil. They expected the gentry, in the form of knights, to control the vermin that would otherwise kill their livestock and devour their crops, and also protect them from enemies. And they expected to enjoy at least some of the fruit of their labours, and the hundred or so holy days in the yearly calendar were indeed holidays when men, women and children would rest and rejoice, and dance and sing, as Langland puts it 'Sing-hey-trolly-lolly!' And what was wrong with that? When modern Technological Man flatters himself that he is so much better off than his forebears he forgets the hundred holy days every year. He forgets the fun and companionship of always working in company with other people, men and women and children, and tumblings in the hay, and playing the bagpipes and singing 'Hey-trolly-lolly!' We have only to look at the peasants who still survive today to realise that life for them is not all toil (no matter how romantic – or anti-romantic – writers describe it). There is plenty of good honest outdoor work – but there is also plenty of sitting and talking outside cafés in the peasant areas of France, or sitting on *charpoys* (string beds) smoking hubble-bubbles in India. I have lived in communities which are in every way the same as medieval peasant communities were, and have always been amazed at how much leisure and spare time there was in them. But modern Western man *likes* to believe that all was hell in the old days – it makes him feel better, and justifies in his mind his own excesses against the rest of Nature. *Anything* is justified if it makes possible the glory that is Life in Birmingham or Pittsburgh today and you wouldn't like to go back to toiling fifteen hours a day for three hundred and sixty-four days a year would you?

Looking back on Medieval times a fair-minded human cannot but deplore the awful inequalities between rich and poor. The cottar would have his hand cut off if he killed a deer – and yet the lords and the king would hunt deer to their hearts' content – indeed it often seems that they found time to do very little else. As Robert Kett wrote in the marvellous manifesto that he published before leading his peasant revolt in 1549:

> Whatsoever fowls of the air or fishes of the water, and increase of the earth – all these they do devour, consume, and swallow up: yea, nature does not suffice to satisfy their lusts, but they seek out new devices, and as it were, forms of pleasure to embalm and perfume themselves, to abound in pleasant smells, to pour sweet things on sweet things. Finally, they seek from all places all things for their desire and the provocation of lust. While we in the meantime eat herbs and roots, and languish with continual labour, and yet are envied that we live, breathe, and enjoy common air!

I admire Kett and have named a son after him, and wish that his revolt had prevailed and not been suppressed by foreign mercenaries who had arquebuses and therefore couldn't be withstood even by desperate and determined men.

But it must be remembered that Kett lived well after the true Middle Ages at a time when the landowners were going mad with greed for money and were turning people off their land in favour of money-making sheep. In the Middle Ages there was no doubt plenty of injustice, and it was quite wrong that the husbandman should not be left with the fruits of his labour, but consider the thing from the point of view of *Nature-not-Man*. If the Great God Pan had lived in England in Medieval times he would have welcomed the severe forest laws, that prevented men from cutting trees and preserved the deer for the King to hunt. For the King and his nobles could have killed very few of them and the woods must have teemed with the 'dappled fools' – no doubt the darlings of the Great God Pan. Forests covered most of the land, wild animals abounded in them, and the clearings that remained were well cultivated, without damaging machines or dangerous chemicals; and men, if they really *wanted* to, could take to the forests, like Robin Hood and his merry men, and poach the King's deer, and rob the rich and give to the poor, and generally have a high old natural time. Mankind was at peace with Nature, and was kept at a proper balance, and his intervention did nothing but good. Child mortality, and the occasional Black Death, kept numbers down within reason, and it was very seldom that famine stalked the land. The Life Force, if it could think, would have felt very pleased with the gentle progress of its new experiment of Man.

Unquestioning belief in religion it was that kept men and women satisfied with their lot, and prevented, for centuries after it could have happened, the attempt of Mankind to 'conquer Nature'. To have thought in terms of 'conquering Nature' in Medieval times would have been considered blasphemous. God had ordained the place of Mankind among the rest of Nature, just as He had ordained the place of each person within the society of which he or she was a part.

It is interesting in this context that in the Islamic world, where the abstract sciences were flourishing and making great progress, people actually drew back, consciously, from the practical developments that this science would have made possible. The ancient Greeks, or the Greeks in Alexandria, made a working steam engine for example. The extremely clever philosophers in the Islamic world still had records of the Alexandrian experiments and could easily have gone ahead and designed a steam engine too. There is evidence that they purposely abstained. They purposely kept their science abstract. It would have seemed to good Muslims blasphemous to have interfered too much with what seemed to them the work and intentions of God.

In Christendom the same scruples were held. It was enough for most men to till the land, hunt, herd beasts, live simply and humbly in small dwellings, worship, feast, procreate, and die. The aristocracy hunted and fought wars, exacted heavy rents from the cultivators; at worst they were brigands – at best protection-racket operators – their deal with the peasant was: 'If you let us take half of what you produce we'll protect you from worse brigands who'll take the lot!' But they, too, thought not at all of seriously trying to 'conquer' Nature. Because of their position in Society they must have thought of themselves as very much the lords of creation but there is no evidence to make one believe that they did not think of themselves as part of that creation too.

It is probably an oversimplification, but it took Galileo, with his telescope and his new vision of the Cosmos, to change all that.

CHAPTER FIVE

Of Renaissance Man and the Reformation

Bitter was it oh to see
The sealy sheepe
Murdered by the ravening wolves
While the sheephards did sleep.
Bitter was it oh to vewe
The sacred vyne
While the gardiners played all close
Rooted up by the swine.
Levell levell with the ground
The towres do lye
Which with the golden, glittering tops
Pearsed once to the sky.
Owles do scrike where the sweetest hymnes
Lately were songe,
Toades and serpents hold their dennes
Where the palmers did throng.
Weepe, weepe, O Walsingham,
Whose dayes are nightes
Blessings turned to blasphemies
Holy deeds to dispites.
Sinne is where our Ladie sate,
Heaven turned is to hell,
Sathan sittes where our Lord did swaye,
Walsingham oh farewell.
Some verses from a poem about the destruction of the holy
shrine of Walsingham, believed to be by Philip Howard, Earl
of Arundel.

They say they can make God of a piece of bread – believe them not!
Last words of John Noyes, shoemaker of Laxfield, as he was
being burned at the stake for being a Protestant.

IT IS STRANGE THAT the discovery that Man's world was not the centre of the Universe was necessary before Man, or many men, decided that the Universe was indeed created just for Man. But it was this discovery, first made by Copernicus and then confirmed by Galileo with his telescope that shook men's faith in the Church. The Church survived the shock, but only by altering its dogmas and therefore demonstrating to all people that it was not, as they had thought, infallible. Darwin's theories had much the same effect on a very different kind of Church over two centuries later.

As long as people believed implicitly that the dogmas of the Church were immutable they were quite happy to accept Mankind's still quite humble place in Nature. Maybe from the point of view of the interests of Nature-not-Man on this planet it would have been better if the Church had succeeded in defending its dogmas, no matter how incorrect these really were. For the great leap forward made by Copernicus and Galileo opened the way to – well, the hydrogen bomb amongst other things. But the truth, as a lot of people have pointed out from time to time, will out. It is no good ever trying to suppress the truth – the thing to do is to try to find the whole truth. If we knew the whole truth we would not make hydrogen bombs: nor nuclear power stations either. If we knew the whole truth we would not try to kick the ladder of Nature from under us! We would realise that we are part of Nature too.

The great changes that came about in Man's attitude to the rest of Nature during the Renaissance occurred in a very small part of the world: in north-western Europe in fact. They only occurred in the Protestant countries. It has only been since the Second World War that countries like Italy, Spain, and the south of France, have begun to make the changes that began in England during Henry VIII's time.

The most important of these changes, from the point of view of Man's relations with the rest of Nature, was the substitution of a money economy for a subsistence one. This could not have happened in a Catholic country. The only reason why it *is* happening so very fast in so-called Catholic countries today is that they are no longer really Catholic.

For the Church taught that men must be contented with their stations in life, must embrace poverty, as their Master did, like a bride, must be content to toil with Mother Earth and must not strive to alter the nature of things, and, most important, must abstain from usury.

Of course the *rich* were different. All they had to do was just go on being rich. It was ordained that they should be rich. They were no doubt put in that happy situation by their Maker. And for this reason they had no motivation for trying to interfere with the world at all. They did not want to drain swamps, cut down forests, evict the peasants to make room for sheep, sink mines or any of these things. They were doing quite nicely thank you as it was. Why worry and fuss about making money? Money came in from their rents. Labour was so cheap that they could have plenty of servants, and what Byron later called his 'makers and unmakers of beds'.

But in those countries of Northern Europe where Luther's unsettling words prevailed everything became open to question. In England Henry VIII kicked out the Pope not for any doctrinal reasons – the last thing he wanted to do was to alter the Church in any way except by making himself head of it. He was after power – not freedom of thought. But he opened floodgates which nothing later could close. Queen Mary tried hard enough to close them with charred flesh but as other tyrants have found before and since, the blood of martyrs cannot quench a revolution.

But Henry VIII, acting as always completely selfishly, simply put an end to the Middle Ages. He dissolved the monasteries so that he could grab their great wealth, keeping as much as he could possibly do with and dishing the rest out to favourites. He thus ensured himself a large body of admirers. Thus was ended a thousand years of slow organic development towards a fruitful and beautiful relationship between Mankind and the rest of Nature – a relationship which was possibly the most pleasing to the Life Force of any that had so far developed on this Earth.

The lands and buildings (certainly the magnificent granges that the monks had scattered about their vast estates to conduct their farming from) and above all the gold and silver, and the lead off the cathedral roofs, could all be used for quite a new purpose – *for making money for rich men.*

This was quite a new motivation. As described above, in feudal Catholic countries rich men just did not need more money. They could do absolutely anything that they wanted with what they had got. But with the overthrow of Catholicism a new spirit came in. Anything goes. Henry VIII created a whole new class – lawyers and politicians and schemers who had come from 'nothing' (as they would have expressed it themselves) and were avid to make money – and more money – and grab more land – and marry money – and land. Like all parvenus they were ruthless, and had none of the feeling of responsibility towards tenants and labourers which was part of the inherited tradition of the old aristocracy, and they set about changing the face of the countryside in the most determined manner.

The great enclosure movement in England was not begun in Henry VIII's time – it had started much earlier, but after the dissolution of the monasteries it went forward apace.

The subsistence husbandry of the old manorial estates had no doubt made a good life for the people involved in it, provided they could content themselves with 'Adams cheer' and simple things, but it did not make *money.* It is probable that many of the peasants of the Middle Ages never handled money at all. The women spun and wove flax, nettles and wool (nettles made a good rough cloth), stored the summer's milk as butter and cheese, salted meat, brewed ale, and the men ploughed and sowed and reaped and no doubt drank the ale.

It is fashionable nowadays to decry the Medieval peasants' life as nasty, brutish and short, but I personally just don't believe it was like that at all. I happen to have lived that kind of life myself for twenty-five years and found it none of these things.

The peasant's life could have been ideal if he had not had to pay rent and tithes. But he carried on his back a vast load of parasites. Half of his produce was simply scooped up by the lord of the manor before he got it off the field – and then ten per cent of the rest by the priest. Much of the time when he could have been working his own land had to be spent in working on the lord's – all for no payment at all. The lord even owned the windmill or watermill and no one was *allowed* to grind his own grain; it had to be done by the lord's miller so that the lord could get his cut out of it. The poor peasant had to pay for *everything* from the sweat of his brow – *everything* – fine horses, all that ermine, rich food, the lot.

I think we can have a very good idea of what a Medieval peasant's life was like by going and living with Medieval peasants of today. I have done just this. I spent a couple of months in the village of Barwasni, near Sonepat, in the Punjab, and also diverse weeks and days in other peasant communities in such countries as Ethiopia (until the Russians came a typical Medieval country), Iran and Sri Lanka, and have a very good idea what the life led in these places was (and still is) like. In every case I found when the cultivators *owned* their land (as my hosts did at Barwasni) life was extremely prosperous and pleasant. Where half or three-quarters of the crop had to go to some parasite of a landlord life was hard and too austere. But even then there was some happiness and jollity and some fun.

This book is about the relationship between Man and Nature-not-Man, but Man's cruelty to his fellows always seems to go hand in hand with his cruelty to the rest of Nature.

Let us hear again the voice of Robert Kett, the leader of the peasant rebellion in East Anglia in 1549, for he expressed so movingly the plight of poor men oppressed by rich ones:

> The pride of great men is now intolerable, but our condition miserable. These abound in delights; and compassed with the fullness of all things and consumed with vain pleasures, thirst only after gain, inflamed with the burning delights of their desires. But ourselves, almost killed with labour and watching, do nothing all our life but sweat, mourn, hunger, and thirst . . .
>
> The present condition of possessing land seemeth miserable and slavish holding it all at the pleasure of great men; not freely, but by prescription, and, as it were, at the will and pleasure of the lord. For as soon as a man offend any of these gorgeous gentlemen he is put out, deprived, and thrust from all his goods . . . The lands which in the memory of our fathers were common, those are ditched and hedged and made several; the pastures are enclosed and we are shut out . . . Shall they, as they have brought hedges about common pastures, enclose with their intolerable lusts also the commodities and pleasures of this life, which Nature, the parent of us all, would have common, and bringeth forth every day, for us, as well as for them? . . . Nature had not envied us other things. While we have the same form, and the same condition of birth together with them, why should they have a life so unlike ours, and differ so much from us in calling?

But man has seldom on this planet been able to free himself from the tyranny of landlordism for quite a simple reason. The man who cultivates the soil has not got time to train himself in arms, nor engage in political intrigue and military self-aggrandisement. The man who lives in the city, or has a base in the city, has. The city-based government can always command weapons and an army. The peasant is defenceless against these things. The city man simply takes what he wants

62

from the peasant by force of arms. If the peasant is lucky a state of affairs is created where at least he knows where he is – he knows he is going to be robbed and left with exactly enough to keep him alive (a dead peasant is no good to anybody) but the robbery will be committed with some pretence of 'law' and decency. Landlordism is a protection racket – the deal is: 'If you let us rob you peaceably we'll stop others from robbing you forcibly!'

Even so, many estates in Medieval times were no doubt managed happily and peacefully, there were plenty of checks and balances in the way of courts-leat, manorial custom, etc., to make sure that life was not too intolerable, and many a lord was kind and humane and felt the same sort of loyalty to his lieges as they were expected to show to him. The intense loyalty of the good infantry officer in a modern army to his men is an example of this kind of relationship. A good platoon commander in the two Great Wars simply would not rest until he had seen to it that the men under his command were as happy as possible and well looked after, and he expected, and got, the same sort of loyalty from them.

But the new *improving* landlords that came in with the Reformation were a different cup of tea altogether. They wanted one thing – and one thing only – *money*. And, in England, the latter meant sheep. Sheep don't require people, except just a shepherd or two to look after them, and some dogs, and gangs of landless vagabonds to come and shear them once a year. So it was out with the peasants. The old open field system simply had to go to make room for sheep. In the days before fences (and remember wire is a very recent invention) sheep just could not exist where there were too many arable fields. Legally or illegally (and certainly quite immorally) the landlords drove the peasants from their land. Gangs of beggars roamed the country, and ultimately many of the displaced people drifted to the towns, which were growing quickly, to work in the new woollen industries which were growing up everywhere (oh yes, there was a flourishing wool trade much earlier than Tudor times, we know – but then it expanded), or in the shipbuilding trades, or iron founding, or glass-making, or the hundred and one industries and trades that grew up with the collapse of the Middle Ages.

From the point of view of Nature-not-Man the Reformation in northern Europe was a disaster. The forests were ruthlessly cut down to provide timber for shipbuilding or charcoal for iron smelting, glass-making and other uses. The forests just melted away. The proliferation of sheep prevented the regeneration of woodlands. The hoof of the sheep was, two hundred years later in England, called 'the golden hoof' – for the good it did when sheep were carefully folded on arable land by good husbandmen. When they were left to roam almost at will over a deserted countryside their sharp hoofs – and their close-cropping teeth – were purely destructive.

But the wool flowed into the weaving sheds, and across to the continent in the form of cloth, and made vast fortunes for the new landlords, while the land eroded and the poor people starved.

It was a completely new *attitude* to Nature-not-Man. The ruthlessness shown by rich men to poor ones was shown in full measure to non-human forms of life too. The oak trees that were cut down in increasing numbers to build the growing fleets of ships that ranged the oceans all ended up as driftwood. The new greed caused war after war and, as the next couple of hundred years went by, vast fleets of ships were created out of murdered oaks to be sent against other vast fleets from other countries and these fleets just hammered each other to pieces with cannon. The cannon, too, were made of iron which had been smelted with charcoal from the same forests, and the very gunpowder was made of the self-same charcoal. People who remembered the love and care bestowed by the monks on forests, orchards, fish-ponds, rivers, and the land, must have watched all this with sadness and dismay.

Queen Elizabeth made England 'great' around the Globe by encouraging navigation, defeating Catholic Europe in the shape of the Spanish Armada, and settling colonists in the Americas. Catholic Portugal and Spain were sowing the seeds of the destruction of the South American ecosystems by sending *conquistadores* to those countries while Britain and Holland (a strong Protestant rival) were serving North America, South Africa, and the East Indies the same way. At first the traders, bandits and settlers made little impact on the Nature-not-Man of the countries they visited, but they were the seeds for a right lot of tares, no matter how long they were to lie dormant.

Reformation was followed by Counter-Reformation, and it looked occasionally as though this might have prevailed. But the ambitious and enterprising were all on the side of 'progress'. King Charles I tried to impede this progress and had his head cut off for his pains; then things really began to move.

The fens were drained and their age-old balance of Nature completely disturbed. Land was being reclaimed from salting and swamp wherever possible. The same thing was happening in the Low Countries even more vigorously. The clearing of forests went on even faster, and so did the enclosures and the driving of people off the land. Mining, both for metals and for coal, began in earnest. The Romans had of course mined for metals and so had people much earlier, but coal was not exploited seriously until after Tudor times. With an increasing population and far less forest coal had to come in. No doubt it helped to save what was left of the woodland, particularly after a method was found of smelting iron with it. Iron, glass and ceramic production take a vast quantity of energy, and, in England, coal came just in time to save the final clearance of the forests.

Meanwhile, what about Man's attitude to Nature-not-Man during all this? What was happening to that? What about his feelings about his own place in the rest of Nature?

There was an immediate and quite dramatic change in the nature of the great buildings in England (which just happens to be the country I know best) after the Reformation.

Two sorts of great buildings have come down to us from pre-Reformation times: castles and churches. The castles were of course built for severely practical purposes: they were mostly constructed by the conquering Normans to keep the Welsh and the English down. (They were not actually *built* by the Normans of course: all conquerers have a happy knack of making the conquered forge their own chains: the English and the Welsh built them, under the lash of the Norman overseer.) As the Normans intermarried and became anglicised they didn't bother to build any more castles, and there is no doubt, if the Medieval system had gone on indefinitely, they would have been quarried for stone and become things of the past. They were no longer necessary.

No, the really *grand* buildings were the churches, and in particular, of course, the cathedrals. These weren't unique to England of course: they were built all over Christendom, and their unity – the fact that new fashions in church building spread so quickly over Europe – shows that Christendom was one.

The great cathedrals are without any doubt the most splendid and magnificent constructions ever erected by Man. Not only are they absolutely enormous – they are superbly delicate and beautiful. It is impossible for modern Man to conceive how they were built. To pile up stone on stone to the dizziest heights – to construct superb arches and vaulting up in what to medieval Man must have seemed the very sky – to embellish every surface with the most fitting and delightful ornament, in perfect taste – one feels that the Medieval master builders could not go wrong. How wrong our modern 'architects' can go!

Contemplate the preparations to build an office block today and those that took place before the building of the Lady Chapel of Ely Cathedral! Before the office block can be built there are years of negotiations, planning authorisations, whole armies of 'architects' and draughtsmen toiling away – thousands and thousands of 'man hours' of it – acres of paper covered with calculations by quantity surveyors, stresses and strains calculated and heaven knows what else. Then come the builders. An army of workers, a great fleet of tipping trucks and dumper trucks, enormous pile-drivers, and drilling machines, hundreds of tons of mild steel reinforcing, thousands and thousands of tons of concrete – enormous tower cranes which one must admit are miracles of ingenuity – and, many, many strikes and labour disputes afterwards, and costs that escalate from day to day because of all sorts of 'unforeseen factors'. Finally we have a building, whether hideous or not we will not go into – all such judgements must be subjective. And the *purpose* of the building? Why to make money for the millionaire who had it built of course – but the practical purpose in the end is for it to be filled, every day, with hundreds of clerks and hundreds of typists, all shuffling bits of paper from one to another.

Now let us see how the Lady Chapel, that superbly beautiful adjunct to Ely Cathedral, was begun. The contemporary *Ely Chronicle* tells us.

Alan of Walsingham, the sacrist (who was later responsible for constructing the new lantern of the cathedral – *four hundred tons of it* spanning a gap of seventy-four feet, eighty-six feet above the floor), discussed the idea of building the Lady Chapel with his assistant Brother John.

Brother John betook himself to prayer, and thereafter called his mates together, some being monks, some, likewise, being

67

seculars. And them he besought to meet at a certain hour, and help him in digging out a square trench which might serve as a foundation for the whole fabric.

At the appointed time, accordingly, they met one night, and began to dig, each one in the place assigned to him . . .

And when the whole night was well nigh spent, and in the earliest dawn, a small rain came on, to the annoyance of those digging. Calling then his mates from their work he said: 'Brethren mine, and fellow labourers, yea, most heartily do I thank you for your long and well-wrought task. And good it is to pause a little after your work. Therefore I commend you to God, and may He pay you a full worthy wage for your labour.'

Consider that oh my masters – and imagine the palaver of commissioning McAlpines to build you a block of flats!

What is the difference? *The medieval builders were building for the glory of God!* Whether God existed or not makes not one jot of difference – He existed for them! They were building for the glory of God. And they felt that God *would* pay them 'a full and worthy wage' for their labour – they were damned sure nobody else would.

In all the ages of Mankind no doubt some people have felt that they were working for the glory of God. Many good craftsmen and artists do even today – even though they think they do not believe in God. Maybe I am writing this book with that motivation. I would like to think so because it won't be worth a damn if I am not. But, not since the Reformation in England has any really large work been built for any other reason than for the aggrandisement of Man.

The new St. Paul's Cathedral, the later Oxford and Cambridge colleges, above all the vast and luxurious mansions that dot our countryside: these were all built for the glory of the man or people who paid for them. Nobody *paid* for the cathedrals – they were 'paid' for with the sweat of honest peasants and craftsmen – and their zeal – and their love. What songs did they sing as they toiled at the crude wooden capstans that hoisted huge blocks of stone two or even three hundred feet into the sky?

And with all our tower cranes, and concrete-mixers, and pre-stressed concrete beams, and modern technology we cannot produce anything like what they produced. For what they built was absolutely superb and will probably never be equalled on this planet in any age nor by any men.

Before the Reformation men built to the glory of God, after it they built for the glorification of Man – it is as simple as that.

And what has all this got to do with Man's attitude to the rest of Nature?

Well, the stage is now set for our next chapter, which I am going to call 'Of the Age of Reason'.

CHAPTER SIX

Of the Age of Reason

*The law and ordinance of nature, under which all men are born, and
for the most part live, forbids* nothing *but what no one wishes, or
is able, to do.*
Spinoza.

IT IS INSTRUCTIVE TO follow the workings of men's minds in the
Europe of the seventeenth and eighteenth centuries.

After over one and a half thousand years of obscurantism
Western Man suddenly found that he could use his *reason,*
untrammelled by religious dogma or fear of Hell.

Of course there was plenty of hanging back. Witness the
professor of philosophy at Padua who refused to look through
Galileo's telescope for fear that he might see the truth through
it. But, after Galileo, philosophical speculation moved from
the Catholic world to the Protestant, and then nothing could
stop it from developing to the state that it has reached today.

At first the philosophers had to claim belief in – and really
did believe in – God, and they took the 'revealed truth' of the
Bible for granted. But they managed to square this position
with their consciences quite easily by saying, simply, that
reason was one thing and faith another. They simply paid
lip-service to faith and then forgot about it. It did not really
come into their philosophical calculations.

Descartes, a Frenchman writing around 1636, came up with the following:

> I perceived it to be possible to arrive at a knowledge highly useful in life; and in room of the *speculative* philosophy usually taught in the schools, to discuss a *practical,* by means of which knowing the force and action of fire, water, air, the stars, the heavens, and of all other bodies that surround us, as distinctly as we know the various crafts of our artisans, we might also apply them in the same way to all the uses to which they are adapted, and thus render ourselves *the lords and possessors of nature.*

The phrase that I have put in italics in this passage is the first reference that I can find in philosophical literature anywhere to the new conception – that Man is apart from Nature and can control and 'conquer' it. Bacon, in England, came near to the same idea in his writings; he wanted 'to extend more widely the limits of the power of greatness of Man'. Descartes, although a self-confessed Catholic all his life, acted like a great charge of dynamite in blowing away centuries of stuffy and dreary scholasticism and in cracking men's faith in revealed religion.

Bacon and Descartes opened the floodgates. Through them came the prophets of the New Age. Hobbes came along surprisingly early, and although he trotted off to church every Sunday like a good boy, wrote that Man had no soul – the mind was purely mechanistic – outside stimuli provoked responses within the brain that caused it to stimulate the body to act in diverse ways.

Spinoza came as near as he could get to becoming an atheist although he, too, managed to pretend to other people at least that he still accepted revealed religion.

Spinoza was an almost perfect example of a new kind of Man. He attched no importance whatever to *feelings* in his thought – he was an extreme example of the person who has developed the left lobe of his brain to the total exclusion of the right, to use the image that we referred to in Chapter 1.

Stuart Hampshire, in his good little book on Spinoza in Everyman's library, points out that Descartes, Leibnitz and Spinoza wrote purposely in Latin, which 'having largely lost its poetical and conversational uses, could be made entirely formal and abstract and . . . extremely clear; words could be given a precise technical meaning, comparatively unconnected with any of their shifting, figurative uses in ordinary speech'.

Scientific truth was to be obtained henceforth only by the use of mathematics. It is marvellous how far mathematics managed to carry on the search for truth about the physical universe – culminating in Einstein who was showing signs, before he died, of being driven, in his search for truth, to call on inspiration – something more than just mathematics – to probe even further. Einstein may have developed the left lobe of his brain to dizzy heights but he was unusual for a Western scientist in that he did *not* totally ignore the use of his right lobe.

As for the first rationalists – their attitude to the hampering right lobe is expressed typically in their attitude to poetry.

John Baptiste Rousseau claimed that Descartes 'cut the throat of poetry'. John Locke, far later, thought that if a child had an aptitude for poetry its parents 'should labour to have it stifled and suppressed as much as may be'. David Hartley said poetry was 'natural enough for the infancy of knowledge in the early Ages of the World' and 'the Pleasures of the Imagination are to Men in the early part of their adult Age, what playthings are to children'.

He also considered that 'most kinds of Musik, Paintings, and Poetry, have close connections with Vice'. 'The polite Arts are scarce to be allowed, except when consecrated to religious purposes.'

John Locke, in England, finally knocked poetry on the head for Descartes' cutting of its throat hadn't quite finished it off!

The new cold philosophy of reason-alone succeeded in the end in completely destroying the union of heart and head (or Right Lobe and Left Lobe if we are to believe that rather unlikely anatomical arrangement) – the synthesis of thought and feeling out of which real poetry has to be born. As Thomas Sprat put it: 'When the fabulous age was past Philosophy took a little more courage; and ventured more to rely upon its own strength, without the Assistance of Poetry.'

As for religion – for all the dreary speculations of those un-utterably dreary people the Schoolmen – Catholic Christianity had retained a warm and loving relationship with the rest of Nature – and still retains it in those small pockets of the world where it survives. The early Christians had had the sense (nay been forced) to take over the myriad tutelary deities of the pagans that came before them and incorporate them in Christian imagery. The thousands of 'Our Lady of . . . This or That' scattered throughout Europe (and Catholic India, South America, and even Japan) are simply old Nature Gods made respectable.

As long as Man recognised such regional deities (for deities they in fact were) he would stay his hand in behaving too ruthlessly towards the rest of Nature. If you really believe that Our Lady of the Fountain haunts a certain dell you cannot move into the dell too ruthlessly with a chain-saw and a bulldozer. The Australian Aborigines fight desperately to preserve parts of what is left to them of their country just because these parts are *sacred places*.

The new Protestant spirit did away with all sacred places. This is Hooker, in his *Ecclesiastical Polity,* on all the creations of the imagination of people who wished to invest some beloved place with some significance:

For being dispersed, some in the air, some on the earth, some among minerals, dens, and caves that are under the earth; they [local spirits] have by all means laboured to effect a universal rebellion against the laws, and as far as in them lieth utter destruction of the works of God. These wicked spirits the heathens honoured instead of gods, both generally under the name of *dei inferni;* and particularly, some in oracles, some in idols, some as household gods, some as nymphs; in a word, no foul and wicked spirit which was not one way or other honoured of men as God, till such time as light appeared in the world and dissolved the works of the devil.

Such thinking led to the ferocious witch-hunts of Puritan days, when poor old women by the hundred were hunted out, accused, tortured and burnt. But, more significantly from the point of view of any Life Force that there might be, it cleared the way for a more ruthless exploitation of Nature-not-Man. Nothing was to get in the way – no love of place, no sentiment – of Descartes' attempt to render ourselves the 'lords and possessors of nature'.

It is interesting, if desperately sad, to stand in the middle of the East Anglian or Hanoverian barley prairie, and, seeing nothing but flat bulldozed land all around you, to think: maybe *here,* where I stand, was the sacred grove of some people, who drew comfort and strength from some friendly local deity long ago.

This brings us to the whole question of whether or not Mankind should continue with the search for truth. If the search for truth leads to evil – should we not abandon it? Before any good rationalist flings this book down in disgust with the intention of never reading another word of it I will say: Of *course* we must go on searching for the truth at all costs and all the time!

But from the point of view of Life-not-Man on this planet (and it looks as though it might be from the point of view of the survival of Man too) it would have been far better if Mankind

74

had never swept aside the pagan Gods at all: at least that is what it seems like in the short-term view.

Maybe if we wish to survive we will have to reinvent this reverence for place – this worship of the spirit that we *feel* inhabits certain localities that are dear to us and that give significance to our existence. (Ah – but did not the Age of Reason destroy *feeling*? We only *think* now, don't we?)

But as for the search for truth – Mankind cannot give this up no matter how much we may want to. When the Life Force evolved/created/dreamt us up it saw to that. No – we can never cease the search for truth. What I am pleading for is that we must carry this search *all the way*. But carry it on with our reason helped by our imagination – with *both* lobes of our brains in fact. And carry it on with humility, and the constant realisation that Nature has shoved us here for a purpose – her purpose – not ours alone.

Montaigne wrote: 'Whoever contemplates our mother Nature in her full majesty and lustre is alone able to value things in their true estimate.' Right on! And Jean Jacques Rousseau:

> It is a noble and beautiful spectacle to see man raising himself, so to speak, from nothing by his own exertions; dissipating, by the light of reason, all the thick clouds in which he was by nature enveloped; mounting above himself; soaring in thought even to the celestial regions; like the sun, encompassing with giant strides the vast extent of the universe; and, what is still grander and more wonderful, going back into himself, there to study man and get to know his own nature, his duties and his end. All these miracles we have seen renewed in the last few generations.

But of course the truth includes far more than just such paltry matters as whether the Earth revolves round the sun or the sun the Earth. All such truth is moving anyway. As Einstein has shown us, all movement is relative. It is just as true to say that the Earth is the one fixed point in the Universe and the whole of the rest of the stuff whizzes round it as to say that the sun is a fixed point in relation to the Earth. Can there be a fixed point in the Universe at all? The early metaphysicians thought there was and it was God.

But we might learn from the Hindu indifference to all such trifling pieces of 'truth'. The Brahmin, learned in the scriptures, just does not care a damn if the sun moves round the Earth or the Earth moves round the sun. He is concerned with far deeper aspects of the truth than that.

In the great Age of Reason all religion was due for the scrap-heap anyway. For a surprisingly long time the new rationalists clung on to some semblance of it. Even David Hume, after thoroughly debunking all Christian and Judaic miracles, wrote: 'Our most holy religion is founded on *Faith,* not on reason; and it is a sure method of exposing it to put it to such a trial [judging it by reason] as it is by no means fitted to endure.' In other words – let us just pretend that we believe all that rigmarole so that we can get on with the task of using our reason – and reason alone.

It was left to the French, where the new Men of Reason found themselves still face to face with all the raw credulity of the unreformed Catholic Church, to throw the baby out with the bathwater.

Holbach, in his *Systéme de la Nature,* claims that *there is nothing behind Nature at all.* It was only because Man did not know Nature enough that he invented God. 'Let us be content to say that matter has always existed, that it moves in virtue of its own essence, and that all phenomena of Nature are due to the different movements of the various kinds of matter of which Nature consists.' Man is purely physical, has no soul, his moral nature is just a part of his physical nature, but we have estranged ourselves from Nature and hence all our ills.

Holbach is always considered one of the first true atheists – but is this atheism at all? Holbach abolished God – but *worshipped Nature*. What is the difference? I have to leave that question for people far more learned in the scriptures than I am to decide.

The early atheists were nothing if not moralists too. Holbach believed that men were neither good nor evil – they are machines, but they are altruistic because if we make others happy we make ourselves happy. It was an atheism of noble aspirations. Man must be taught that behind Nature there is nothing and thus shall Man learn to depend only upon himself and his good brain, and it is up to *him* – and him alone – to make himself virtuous. Virtue for its own sake, with no thoughts of reward or punishment in Heaven or in Hell. The new atheism spread all throughout the Western world, and is now the official religion of a large part of it (the peoples of the USSR and its new colonies) and is indeed believed by far the greater part of educated Western Man. What, I ask again, makes so-called Christians so very reluctant to die?

By my terms of reference in this book I am only interested in atheism – or any other system of thought – by trying to judge its effect, for good or for evil, on the rest of Nature: Nature-not-Man. Or Nature-including-Man if you like.

Well, has atheism operated for good or for ill?

This question is disallowed. It is not permitted to advocate the retention of a belief, or its rejection, on the grounds of whether it will have a good result or not. The only permissible criterion for assessing the truth is – is it true? Is it true that there is no God? If our reason – ay and our hearts – lead us to believe that this is true, then we must believe it even if the belief leads to the destruction of the Universe! We must find out if any given belief is true – not whether it is expedient. There are people today (and people I admire) who wish us all to rejoin the Catholic Church – because if we did it would save Nature and Mankind. I think, if we could, it might, indeed it probably would. But I am not for this reason going to join the Catholic Church. If I do, as I probably shall, it will be for other reasons. Because, endeavouring to retain my honesty and integrity, I will not believe anything, or even kid myself that I believe anything, because it would be expedient to do so. If Mankind goes on believing there is no God he will probably end up by destroying all Life on this planet. But this fact is no argument for making us start again believing in God. I cling fast to the Hindu belief that the *ends do not justify the means.* If I have to adopt the *means* of 'believing' what I really do not believe in order to achieve the *end* of saving Life on this Earth then I am afraid Life will have to go. The truth is more important to me (and to every honest person I believe) than Life on this or any other planet – it is the only thing that is really important at all.

Let us then go on searching diligently (because the lives of our posterity depend on it) for the *whole* truth. The early rationalists did right to sweep away superstition. They did right to search for the truth. They were right, considering the evidence, to arrive at the conclusions they did arrive at. The conclusions though were not necessarily right.

I think they were wrong to make use of one half of their beings only, and the fact that they did so – that they 'cut the throat of poetry' – made them arrive at wrong conclusions. But let us be grateful that they cleared away a lot of rubbish and left the way open for people who came after to carry on the search – the search that it is obviously the destiny of Man to conduct – for the truth, the whole truth, and nothing but the truth. We should be content with nothing less than that.

CHAPTER SEVEN

Of Industrial Man: The Land

We of the nineteenth and twentieth centuries have the unenviable distinction of having created the first ugly civilisation in the long history of mankind. The industrial age has brought innumerable benefits, but it has created an environment for man that is visually little short of a nightmare.
Sir John Rothenstein, Letter to The Times, 20 February 1965

AND WHAT OF THE hoi polloi during this splendid Age of Reason? Well James Thomson describes their position quite succinctly in some of his plodding verse:

While thus laborious crowds
Ply the tough oar, Philosophy directs
The ruling helm.

Bags to be a philosopher.

This book is not about Man's inhumanity to Man *except in so far as Man is part of Nature.* It is just as anti-Life Force to be nasty to a person as to be nasty to a tree.

Throughout the seventeenth and eighteenth centuries enclosure of lands had gone on remorselessly in England, more and more people had been flung out of their holdings, more and more the land was being farmed to make money –

and generally to make money for people who already had too much. It was the landlords who made the money of course, not the farmers, and certainly not the farm labourers.

Very few writers noticed the plight of the displaced peasantry. Cobbett did though.

> The labourers looked miserably poor. Their dwellings are little better than pig-beds, and their looks indicate that their food is not nearly equal to that of a pig. Their wretched hovels are stuck upon little bits of ground *on the road side,* where the space has been greater than the road demanded. In many places they have not two rods to a hovel. It seems as if they had been swept off the fields by a hurricane and had found shelter under the banks by the road side! Yesterday morning was a sharp frost; and this had set the poor creatures to digging up their little plots of potatoes . . . And this is 'prosperity' is it?

Cobbett weighed in again and again and again against the 'Bullfrogs' as he called them – the grasping rural capitalists who farmed the land (or had it farmed for them) for nothing else except *money.* It was only where the land was rough and much cut-up by forests that the landlords and big farmers had not been able to get their greedy mitts on everything: In a forested area, 'The labouring people looked pretty well. They have pigs. They invariably do best in the *woodland* and *forest* and *wild* countries. Where the mighty grasper has *all under his eye* they can get but little.'

And what of our concern – what of the effect of all this on Nature-not-Man? Well – not absolutely disastrous yet but pretty damned bad. For it eventually led to monoculture.

The peasant who has to grow all his requirements for food and clothing off his piece of land – or the self-sufficient village community for that matter – is constrained to husband land, crops and animals in an organically sound way. He cannot

80

practise monoculture – the growing of only one crop – even if he wants to.

The new type of commercial farmer – Cobbett's 'bullfrog' or 'mighty grasper' – found which was the most profitable crop to grow and eventually grew nothing but that. I shall try to explain why it was a couple of hundred years after the start of the Industrial Revolution before he *could* do that – but he did it in the end.

This is not supposed to be a book about farming, but farming has got to come into it because it is the most important expression of Man towards Nature-not-Man.

It is useful sometimes, in order to clarify thinking, to pretend things; just as we pretended in this book that there was an unimaginably large man with a long white beard and a very loud voice playing with the stars. Let us now pretend that all Life on this planet is one organism. As the Gaia hypothesis now suggests Terrestrial Life is one *being*.

This is not as ridiculous as it sounds. Consider you from the point of view of a cell in your left kidney, or one of the white blood corpuscles that swim with perfect free will in your blood. The cell in your kidney cannot move (unless all of you moves) but it can move as an oak tree can move. The white blood cell can move a lot – in fact to it, its world is vast. These cells are just as much individual animals as you think you are. They would look upon you, if they could see and think, just as you look upon all Life on Earth.

Now imagine you are in just such a relationship to Life on Earth. You are simply one of the cells that make up an organism. The organism is a funny shape – it is the surface of a sphere. But it might be argued that *you* are a funny shape. I certainly am.

Now it could be imagined that you are just one of the cells in the world brain. It might be that all we thinking animals are cells which make up the brain of the world organism. We react together as the cells in our brains do. We act on the non-brain part of the world-organism as the cells of our own brains react on our left legs.

Like the cells of our own brains the cells of the world brain are there *for the benefit of the whole organism.* If the cells of my own brain start ignoring, neglecting, or abusing, the non-brain cells of my body – neglecting their interests in any way in fact – I shall simply come to a stop. I have a very lively appreciation of the fact that the good of all the cells in my body is the good of each one of them.

Outside the window of my house is a rambling rose that threatens to take over the building completely, which was planted by one of my Welsh predecessors here. Then there is a big vine with no grapes which I planted myself, then an elder tree (unhappy is the homestead that does not have an elder tree growing near it) then a herb garden, then rank on rank of alder, ash, oak, willow and hazel trees – all marching, it sometimes appears to me, on me and this house. Then come the mountain heather and dwarf gorse.

I have to – and I have a right to – contain and control all this life, otherwise it would take my farm completely over and leave no room for me. But, supposing I am just a cell in the world brain, and all these trees and bushes and herbs and all the rest of it are cells in the world body. Have I the right ruthlessly to destroy all these other cells of the body of which I am part?

When the brain cells in a human body get unbalanced and out of kilter the body gets ill and we say the person has 'got cancer'. We cut him about a bit and subject him to damaging radiation and by and by he dies, often extremely unpleasantly. So it behoves our brain cells to behave themselves and do their business properly, and, each one of them, remember that it is there for the good of all not just for the good of itself.

We individual brain cells of the world body should remember the same thing.

And the vile and unmentionable crime of *monoculture* is more than a cancer in the Life-organism that surrounds the world. As it spreads it can be said that the world organism is becoming sick. Its brain cells are not working properly.

Well we have had a flight of fancy. Quite possibly the Life around our planet can *not* be considered as one living organism. But such flights of fancy can be useful sometimes – lateral thinking in the jargon of our times.

The discovery of the use of *coal* was like opening Pandora's box. It was rubbing some magic lamp and summoning up a powerful and dangerous genie.

Life on Earth had, almost one feels of a purpose, stashed away a vast store of energy in Carboniferous times for some future period in which Life itself had developed to the state at which it could put it to some special use. It was like a young man working hard to accumulate capital so that, in his middle age, he could start a business.

People had been nibbling at the coal seams for several centuries before, in the late eighteenth century, they went at it in earnest. At first the development of coal did nothing but good to Nature-not-Man – and to Man himself. For one thing, it saved what was left of the forests. In the 1780s it was discovered that you could smelt iron with coke instead of charcoal and this discovery as much as anything saved what was left of the forests of Europe.

But with ever-increasing speed the lid of Pandora's box was opened and out flew a myriad of weird creatures. Stephenson's 'Rocket' was one of them.

At first the farmers did not derive much benefit – or do themselves or the rest of Life much harm – by the use of the insects that fluttered out of Pandora's box. Coal power was of very limited use in agriculture. It was a hundred years after the invention of the steam engine before a few great heavy monsters began to lumber out onto the fields – traction engines that hauled gangs of ploughs backwards and forwards over the land on endless wire ropes. They would never have knocked out the horse. The threshing machine, driven by steam, came to replace the man with a flail quite early, and thank God for that, many an old man with creaking joints must have said.

And farm labour remained very very cheap. Right up until the Second World War it was the horse and the man that cultivated the soil of England, and it was well after that war that these two power sources were replaced in the rest of Europe.

So the farmers of the Industrial Revolution period could not do too much damage to the rest of Life no matter how much they wanted to. They simply did not have the power or the machinery.

Huge deposits of old bird droppings were discovered in Chile and Peru, and half the sailing ships in the world were employed carrying this 'nitrate' half way round the world so that it could be dumped on the fields of northern and western Europe: mostly England and Germany. This was almost as big a bonanza as coal. I would put the staggering population explosion in England in the nineteenth century almost entirely to the credit – or discredit – of Chilean nitrate. The land suddenly became capable of growing much larger crops.

Before that there had been the improving farmers – Coke of Norfolk and 'Turnip' Townshend and others like them. They had discovered and developed principles of good husbandry that enabled good crops to be grown consistently and year after year. The husbandry of 'high farming' that they developed seems to *me* to have been pretty good for Nature-not-Man – the Chilean nitrate was too much of a forced draught.

Then the white man swarmed out over the hot countries – and the southern countries and the western countries – of the world and began to farm them on a huge scale and with purely extractive methods. It was this 'colonial' farming that was the forcing ground of things like the tractor, the combine harvester and chemical agriculture.

For example, all forms of life on the great prairies of central Canada were destroyed to make room for one species: wheat. If terrestrial life was indeed one organism how did the organism like that? Similar things happened to the Great Plains of the United States, the pampas of South America, the veld of southern Africa and the outback of Autralia.

If you fly in an aeroplane over the middle of Canada and the United States (I did a while back, flying straight from San Francisco) you look down at an interminable chequcr-board of *squares*. The whole country for hour after hour after hour of flying at – what is it, six hundred miles an hour? – is nothing else, just squares. No woods, no bison, no Red Indians, no scrub or bush – just squares. In the north the squares grow wheat – in the middle maize. An increasing number of squares grow nothing at all. Assuredly, whatever else the white man did to North America, he succeeded in turning it into the most *boring* country on Earth and probably among the stars. Both wheat and maize are now the victims of an ever-increasing host of pests and diseases (ever the result of monoculture) but an armoury of poisonous chemicals is sprayed on them – up to a dozen sprays a year in some places – and so far the pests and diseases have been kept in check. But who was the old Roman who said, *'Naturam expellas furca tamen usque recurret'* (If you chuck Nature out with a pitchfork she always returns)? I like my own free translation: If you chuck Nature out of the door she comes back through the window. Consider that statement, oh agricultural chemists and all-conquering agribusiness-men! A deist might put it another way: God is not mocked. Not for too long, anyway. And it may be the longer our agribusinessmen get away with it the harder will be the fall.

Probably Western Man (particularly British Man) was so busy all during the nineteenth century cultivating an overwhelming feeling of superiority over his fellow men in other parts of the world (the 'lesser breeds without the Law' – which included nearly everybody) that he did not have time to worry much about the rest of Nature. Nature was still pretty awesome to nineteenth century Man. And it still seemed pretty enormous.

To illustrate this I can record my own reactions to the Burmese teak and bamboo jungle when I was in it during the Second World War. To me that jungle seemed absolutely enormous and immutable – it might have covered the Earth. Man, I believed then, could never make any mark on it. It was huge and hostile and unmanageable and – I might as well come out with it – *boring*. It just went on and on for too long and was too hostile an environment for me, or in fact for most mammals. (The latter feeling might have been influenced by the fact that there were several hundred thousand enemy soldiers in it – all bent on killing me.)

I had never seen a chain-saw then. I was still, so far as clearing jungles was concerned, a nineteenth-century man. I could imagine rubber planters coming if we were perhaps lucky enough to win the war, and clearing a few thousand-acre patches here and there, using the Naga tribesmen and their little axes, but I could not imagine any human agencies making more than the slightest and most marginal impression on that never-ending hostile forest.

Now of course the case is far different. For we are now living in the world described in Chapter 9 – the Technological Revolution. I have seen five enormous tracked tractors, four of them towing a battleship's anchor-chain behind them, cutting a swathe a hundred yards wide through heavy jungle at Gal Oya in Sri Lanka and going as fast as a man could walk. The Japanese are at this moment negotiating with every Far Eastern government that has jungle in its land for permission to cut the jungle down – every bit of it – for chipboard manufacture. If present tendencies go on the Burma jungles will vanish like snow in a heatwave in a few decades, and every other forest and jungle in the world with them. The Brazilian rain forest is being burnt at an increasing rate. And if humans are the cells of the brain of our world organism the forests are its lungs, for the trees lock up carbon dioxide and enable us to breathe. But alas – the brain has gone mad. Unless this madness can be cured the world organism is doomed.

And what of philosophy – that was 'directing the ruling helm' during the period of the Industrial Revolution? The mainstream of it simply carried on the rationalist movement of the previous century to its logical conclusion. Jeremy Bentham and J.S. Mill are generally considered pretty central to philosophy in Britain during that period and they were never concerned with Nature-not-Man at all – their whole concern was trying (with complete lack of success from my viewpoint at least) to justify *being good* and *being an atheist*. Why, if there was no hope of Heaven nor fear of Hell, should man be good to his neighbours? Well, there was a lot to be said about it and they said a lot. Of course it's not enough to say that if you are nasty to your neighbour he may be nasty to you and therefore it won't pay you to be nasty. Caligula was very nasty to his neighbours and none of them succeeded in being nasty to him until the end. It is quite possible – if you are powerful enough – to be nasty as the devil and get away with it!

But J.B. and J.S.M. were honest men and they were not going to *pretend* they believed in Heaven and Hell just because it made for a happier universe. So they invented the law of 'the greatest good for the greatest number' and that became a very comforting philosophy.

As for their attitude to Nature-not-Man they never thought about it at all. The new huge cities made it possible to be completely unaware and oblivious about Nature-not-Man. Karl Marx, who spent most of his life in the reading room of the British Museum Library, probably came as little into contact with Nature-not-Man as it was possible to do and still stay alive. The result was that *his* philosophy ignored everything not human absolutely completely. He was aware (just) that food came from the country. He was aware that there must be some people out there somewhere who grew it. It was his object to rescue these imaginary people from what he called 'the idiocy of rural life'. (What is that to the idiocy of spending all your life in the British Museum Library?) His idea was to turn peasants into factory workers – and farms into factory floors. His methods have since been tried in Russia, with the result that the country with the greatest continuous wheat-growing area in the world has to import wheat.

But all through the Industrial Age there were voices raised against the *spiritus mundi* – the mainline thinking of the times. Coleridge, Wordsworth, Blake – the poets made a comeback in a limited way; they were *tolerated* by the Victorians like licensed jesters or clowns. After the logical, passionless, witty, sensible, rational and utterly boring verse of the eighteenth century a few people reacted and allowed their hearts to be heard – their right lobes if you like. Being sensible men they could not accept the whole outworn fundamentalist thing again – but they turned to Nature, which they could believe in (it was there) and they invoked the name of God to explain what they saw. Their new God was a pantheistic God – the God of Nature. Not everybody spent all his time in the British Museum Library and you *cannot* be in intimate contact with Nature-not-Man – you cannot stride over the fells of the Lake District or the Quantock Hills or the Alps with the wind in your face and the sun on your back – without feelings of reverence and awe. Listen to Thomas Carlyle.

> Often also I could see the black Tempest marching in anger through the distance: round some Schreckhorn, as yet grim-blue, would the eddying vapour gather, and there tumultuously eddy, and flow down like a mad witch's hair; till, after a space, it vanished, and, in the clear sunbeam, your Schreckhorn stood smiling grim-white, for the great fermenting vat and laboratory of an Atmosphere, of a World, O Nature! – Or what is Nature? Ha! why do I not name thee GOD? Art thou not the 'Living

Garment of God'? O Heavens, is it, in very deed, HE, then, that ever speaks through thee; that lives and loves in thee, that lives and loves in me?

And listen to this – declaimed with a fine Scottish accent.

> Fore-shadows, call them rather fore-splendours, of that Truth, and beginning of Truths, fell mysteriously over my soul. Sweeter than Dayspring to the Shipwrecked in Nova Zembia; ah, like the mother's voice to her little child that strays bewildered, weeping, in unknown tumults; like soft streamings of celestial music to my too-exasperated heart, came that Evangel. The Universe is not dead and demoniacal, a charnel house with spectres; but godlike and my Father's!

Carlyle, and his successors, did not go back to Christianity. Their God was not the God of the Jews – but a God of all the Universe – of all of Nature – of the sublime. Even if some of this school paid lip-service to Christianity they made very little of Christ. But they worked out for themselves perhaps, much as I have tried to do in my own blundering way in the first chapters of this book, that there could not have been a beginning, there can never be an end, there must have been some *tendency* to produce matter out of nothing, life out of matter, etc. etc., otherwise there would be no matter – no life. And that there is – 'I prove it thus!' as Dr. Johnson said as he stubbed his toe.

After casting all sorts of doubts on the existence of such things as Heaven and Hell Carlyle goes on to say:

> All this has vanished, or has not vanished; believe as thou wilt as to all this. But that an Infinite or Practical Importance, speaking with strict arithmetical exactness, an INFINITE, has vanished or can vanish from the Life of any Man; this thou shalt not believe! O brother, the Infinite of Terror, of Hope, of

Pity, did it not at any moment disclose itself to thee, indubitable, unnameable? Came it never, like the gleam of PRETERnatural eternal Oceans, like the voice of old Eternities, far-sounding through thy heart of hearts? Never? Alas, it was not thy Liberalism, then; it was thy Animalism! The Infinite is more sure than any other fact. But only men can discern it; mere building beavers, spinning arachnes, much more the predatory vulturous and vulpine species, do not discern it well!

But the building beavers and the spinning spiders were too busy spinning their industrial webs and felling the forests to build their industrial dams, to bother about the Infinite! They saw infinite wealth in front of them, and that was the only infinite thing they cared about. Oh yes they went to church all right. The Victorians were great churchmen. But, as I've pointed out before, these great churchmen, although supposed to believe in Heaven as a reward for virtue, were mortally afraid to die.

And slowly the Victorian Britons, and to a lesser extent people of other 'advanced' European nations, spread out across the world, and with the hand axe, the horse plough, the breech-loading rifle, the combine harvester drawn by thirty horses, the cheap and sometimes slave labour of blacks, and yellows, and browns, they hacked into the forests, wiped out the wild game to make way for cattle, ploughed up the wild grasses to make way for wheat, ripped open Mother Earth to obtain her riches.

I once worked in an African copper mine. I was a trammer in 650 North level at Mindola Mine, N'kana, in case any old Copperbelt hand wants to know. I went into the smelting house, on the surface, just out of interest. This was an enormous building, like a cathedral, but built, not of carved stone, but of rusty corrugated iron, and *not* built to the glory of God at all! High up above our heads there was a crane. This ceaselessly, night-shift and day-shift, picked up huge trees that had been cut from the jungle, and slung them, branches, leaves, and all, into the furnace in which the copper was being smelted. This was necessary because the carbon produced did something to the copper – purified it in some way or other. Don't tell me how – I don't want to know. As the trees went down towards that fiery hole they burst into flames well before they got there – the heat was so tremendous. A tree is a mass of living creatures of course: it is a whole biological world in itself. Oh I know – I burn wood in my stove and no doubt many an earwig goes in there to its doom. But maybe *scale* has something to do with it. The sight of it horrified me.

We used things called *cheesa*-sticks to light our fuses with, down the mine. They were like small fireworks – you lit them from the flame of your carbide lamp and then lit the fuses with them. When you did this you shouted *cheesa*! which is the word for fire in kitchen-kaffir and everybody got out of the way.

I used to travel the five miles from where I lived to Mindola Number One Shaft on an empty ore train every day. One day we were sitting there, half a dozen of us whites, and one miner, an Afrikaner as it happened (a Dutch-speaking South African white man) kept throwing lighted *cheesa*-sticks into the tinder-dry African forest. Every time he threw one he shouted *cheesa*! and laughed. Great fires were started of course, which probably burnt for days – maybe weeks. When I went back at the end of that shift the fires were out of sight but the whole world was blackened and stinking of smoke. Oh yes – I remonstrated with the man of course. But I was a twenty-three-year-old learner-miner – he was a forty-year-old stoper and he, and the other old miners in the empty box car soon shut me up. 'What – fucking Africa?' said the *cheesa*-stick thrower. 'Like to burn the whole bloody place up, man. Best thing that could happen to it. This country up here belongs to bloody niggers anyway. Like to burn it up and them too!'

I just mention this little incident because I believe it gives a good idea of the new attitude – post-Rationalist, post-

Industrial Revolution – to the rest of Life on this planet: to Nature-not-Man. Extreme perhaps, but not untypical.

In the settled countries with older civilisations, such as England, a country I know well, there was a much more benign attitude during the Industrial Revolution to Nature-not-Man. This was partly due to the successful industrialists' passion for pheasant, grouse and partridge shooting, for hunting, and other rural pursuits. Nearly all the land was held in big estates. Food growing was not really considered of prime importance; were not the wheat prairies of Canada – the beef-rearing pampas of the Argentine – the sheep ranges of Australia absolutely inexhaustible? What was important was to have a 'good showing' of pheasants during the days in each winter when you invited your more influential neighbours, and business associates to shoot them. Why – if you had a title, and could put enough pheasants over the guns in a day so that they could slaughter five or six thousand of these stupid birds before the day was done, you might even lure the Prince of Wales to attend one of your drives and then indeed you had nothing else to live for. It was all downhill from there.

But the result of all this was that the countryside was left fairly well unraped. Plenty of 'coverts' (pieces of woodland) were left for birds and foxes, much woodland was spared which would otherwise have been cut down, hedges were left, wetlands were undrained to encourage snipe and duck. The hunting craze among the rich, stupid though it was, at least prevented the rape of the countryside for another century or so. It was not until the Technological Revolution that the attitude of Man to Nature-not-Man became unrelievedly evil.

We all know about the fate of the bison in North America – when special trains used to carry hundreds of armed 'sportsmen' out into the prairie to slaughter and slaughter just for the sake of satisfying an apparently insatiable blood-lust. A colonel of the United States cavalry, Richard Irving Dodge, who wrote a book called *The Hunting Grounds of the Great West* in 1878, describes very vividly this extermination. He tried to obtain the figures for the number of 'buffalo robes' (bison skins) carried by the United States railways in a year and was met with a blank refusal to disclose the figures. Why? Because in the words of the gallant colonel, 'I am constrained to believe that the refusal is prompted by fears that publicity in the matter might result in some legislation which would interfere with profits.' He is describing the same force of insensate commercial greed which prompts the modern whaling companies to obstruct every attempt at reaching agreement to save the last of the whales. What – not be able to kill the *last one*. He does, however, come up with the figure, arrived at by fairly careful investigation, that in the years 1872-74 four and a half million buffalo were slaughtered for their pelts. Quite a trade grew up in buffalo tongues, which were expensive and easily transported and thousands were shot for this alone, not even the skins being taken off them. The buffalo, minus tongue, was simply left to rot in the prairie. When the book was written four years later the colonel was able to record: 'The buffalo are virtually exterminated. No legislation, however stringent or active, could now do anything either for or against the trade of the "buffalo product".' Although the Colonel plainly did not want the buffalo to be exterminated he cheerfully recounts how he shot hundreds with his own rifle, and on one occasion sent a troop of his own cavalry out to slaughter several hundred for the amusement of an English hunter who was his guest.

This merry jamboree could not go on, and it was the Industrial Revolution that changed it all in the shape of the railways. After splendid descriptions of the life in the prairie 'surrounded on all sides by treacherous savages, by danger of every kind, each man became a host in himself', he mournfully adds:

Now all is changed. There is no longer an unknown. Railroads have bared the silent mysteries of the plains to the inspection of every shopboy. Civilisation like a huge cuttlefish, has passed its arms of settlements up almost every stream, grasping the land, killing the game, driving out the Indian, crushing the romance, the poetry, the very life and soul out of the 'plains', and leaving only the bare and monotonous carcase.

And now all those squares.

In southern Africa it was the same story. The grassveld of the Orange Free State and the Transvaal, and the Karoo veld of the Cape, were, when the first white men arrived, teeming with game. Early travellers write of herds of *trek-bokke* (the migratory springbok) stretching as far as the eye could see. When I went to South Africa in 1934 there was no wild game at all in the Karoo or grassveld, except where a small handful of enlightened farmers had preserved some springbok for the sport of occasionally shooting a few. When I moved up to the bush country of northen South West Africa, a country which had only just been opened up for white settlement, I found still plenty of gemsbok (oryx), springbok, kudu, steenbok and duiker. My boss, an English-speaking South African, was careful that we should not kill too many (he didn't know that Joseph and I used to go and get the odd one occasionally with Joseph's spear) but our Afrikaans neighbours were completely ruthless about hunting. They seemed as though they could never rest until the last buck in the land had been hunted down. The buck are all gone now.

I walked up to a huge flat area of country known as the Etosha Pan, with, as it happened, my friend Joseph. We had two pack donkeys with us to carry water and food. We saw *thousands* of hartebeest and wildebeest (gnu). In the distance they looked like balloons in the heat of the day, suspended in the air above the horizon. This was due to the heat mirage. When I paid a visit to my old boss after the War, I was told they had nearly all gone.

During the years I lived and worked in Northern Rhodesia (now called Zambia) I managed to feed my crew of twenty-four porters and four other servants unfailingly on the meat of the reed buck, kudu, sable, roan, waterbuck, steenbuck, eland, buffalo, lechwe and perhaps a dozen other species. There was no feeling that by shooting one a day one was in any way endangering species. I never shot an elephant (and never will) but I have sat outside my tent eating breakfast and watching over a hundred of them bathing in a little river just below me.

But the British Raj, which ruled that country then, was careful to keep the game slaughterers out of it. I shot because it was my job to shoot (I had to feed my men and was expected to) but very few white people were allowed into the country at all. The white miners of the Copperbelt were carefully controlled as to shooting and didn't they resent it! Only a handful of black men were allowed rifles – a few chiefs and headmen. Now of course thousands of Zambians have rifles and it will only be a matter of time before all the four-footed game is destroyed. To its great credit the Zambian government is trying hard to maintain game reserves but it is an impossible task.

In other places it is worse. Only recently a helicopter survey of the elephant forests of Uganda reported that, as far as the surveyors could see, the Ugandan elephant is now extinct. All they could find were thousands of rotting carcasses. The price of ivory is the cause, and the gangs of armed men left as a legacy by that savage clown Idi Amin, and deserters from the Tanzanian army that went in to fight them.

The Chinese belief that powdered rhinoceros horn is an aphrodisiac has all but exterminated the rhino in Africa, and the world. Unless some can be bred in zoos, or the Chinese be rid of this ridiculous superstition, the rhinoceros will become extinct. The Arab belief that it is 'macho' to wear a dagger with a rhino horn handle is another strong factor for extermination.

These latter excesses of Mankind I cannot lay at the door of the Industrial Revolution: they really belong later. The slaughter by white men of American bison and the game herds of South Africa was certainly one of the results of the Industrial Revolution era but the modern phenomenon of Bronze Age and Iron Age Man roaming the bush with machine-guns is a product of our own – the Technological Age, just as was the Iraq-Iran War.

CHAPTER EIGHT

Of Industrial Man:
The Sea

We must rage against this dying. Machine oil, lipstick, piano keys, whale meat. Will we now say no and begin to heal this terrible ravaging sickness: refuse the products, appeal to those nations who will not see the blood on their hands, make peace with ourselves and eliminate the vessels of war (some as big as football pitches) which parade invisible, ominous, signalling their menace through the world of the whales. Can we begin to forgive ourselves our shameful past and acknowledge the truth:

> *'Blue seas cover seven*
> *tenths of the Earth's surface,*
> *And are the domain of the*
> *largest brains ever created,*
> *With a fifty-million-year-old smile.'*

From Rebecca Hall's review of *Whale Nation* by Heathcote Williams in *Resurgence (Nov–Dec 1988).*

T HE STORY OF MAN'S relationship with the life of the seas in the Industrial and Technological era is as bad or even worse than the story of his relationship with the creatures of the dry land.

It took a long time for the steam engine to take to the waters, and right up until the beginning of our century sail was still important. I learnt to trawl in a Colchester sailing smack, the engine of which was never used (in fact it didn't work). Fishing was carried on under sail and oar until well into the second half of the nineteenth century, and as long as this was so the fish stocks could not be very badly depleted.

The impression one gets from reading accounts of all the fisheries in the early part of the nineteenth century is that there were fish aplenty. For a long time fishermen resisted the trawl net. All during the Middle Ages the trawl – a net bag that is dragged along the sea bed – was not allowed. It was considered that it did too much damage to the sea bottom: such was the reverence for life and the environment at that time. Fishing was by hook and line, by seine nets which were dragged from the shore along a beach, by drift nets, which catch the larger fishes by their gills and let the small ones through, and by other 'engines' which did little damage to the fish stocks. That sort of fishery would have been sustainable for ever.

Even in the Middle Ages ships were sailing from English ports to Iceland with fish-wells – holds which were connected to the sea through perforated plates. Cod were caught on hand lines and placed living in the fresh sea water of these flooded fish holds and taken living back to port. Long before Christopher Columbus European ships were sailing to Newfoundland to catch cod and cure them by salting. These voyages do not appear in our history books because fishermen do not care to publicise their doings. Right back to time immemorial, thousands of herring drifters used to converge on the East Anglian ports to catch herring with drift nets: in 1913 a thousand drifters, sail and steam, were fishing from Great Yarmouth alone. The fish were salted and sent back to the Continent where they formed a great part of the diet of poor people. Because only the drift net was used this fishery too would have been sustainable for ever.

Then, in the mid-nineteenth century, came the great sailing *trawlers*. These were large and powerful sailing ships, sailing from Brixham, Barking near London, Ramsgate, Lowestoft and Yarmouth and later Grimsby, and they dragged their huge beamed trawls over the sandy bottom of the Channel and the North Sea. Fishing ground after fishing ground was discovered and exploited but at first the fish seemed inexhaustible. But Man, for the first time, really set about the denizens of the deep in a destructive manner. A system of *fleet fishing* was developed – the trawling fleets stayed at sea for months at a time and transferred their catches to fast cutters, with ice, which sailed them back to Barking or Grimsby.

Steadily, with sail-power alone, the huge shoals of cod and haddock in the North Sea became eroded. Perhaps they would never have been completely destroyed but then came steam, and made the hunt even more relentless and now the huge diesel stern-trawlers are completing the job.

The tragedy of the sea fisheries is what has been called the 'tragedy of the commons'. On the mountain common land which I can see from my window as I write a number of farmers have rights of commonage. If they are not controlled as to the number of sheep they put on the mountain they put too many. They *have* to. If Dai, who puts a thousand, knows it is too many and cuts his thousand to five hundred, he knows perfectly well that his neighbour Mervyn will shove another five hundred on to make up for it. Dai gains nothing by limiting his stocking rate or exercising self-restraint, so no commoners ever exercise self-restraint. They can't.

I have heard Channel fishermen, who are using the new and terribly destructive twin-boom trawling on the sole grounds – a method they *know* is going to destroy the fishing grounds – lament that they would love to stop doing it but can't. 'What's the good of *me* stopping? The others won't. I've got to compete with the others to make a living. There's hardly any sole left anyway – the only way we can get 'em is to plough the bottom. I'm like the old whore – I know it's wrong but I can't give it up!' That's what a Brixham fisherman said to me.

But, by and large, the fishing grounds were not too badly depleted by the sailing vessels of the Industrial Revolution period. And it was the same with whaling. The Greenland whale, true enough, was rendered pretty scarce by the British, Dutch and Norwegian sailing whalers by 1850, but the great sperm whales, and the whales that ranged the southern oceans, remained numerous.

With the coming of steam at sea the pace altered. Steam-driven factory ships, with fleets of steam catchers, cruised after the whales and first steam drifters and then steam trawlers chased them. Now of course, in our marvellous Technological Age, it is only a matter of time – and a short time – before most species of whales become extinct and a little longer before they all do.

The whaling fleets have helicopters, echo-sounders, electrocuting harpoons, high explosives and God knows what to hunt the last of the leviathans in the furthest reaches of the oceans. Nothing can save them. The purse-seine net has wiped out the herring in the North Sea beyond recall (only a few 'longshoremen' still creep along near the shore).* The mackerel of the Western Ocean are going the same way. When I first came to Wales, sixteen years ago, I could easily go and catch five hundred mackerel in an afternoon on hooks and line. Now I get twenty if I am lucky. *That* kind of fishing would never have destroyed them. It is the giant midwater trawlers, from a dozen nations, often with attendant factory ships, that are doing it. Government regulations do not help. There is a quota now for landing mackerel. The giant ring-nets used encircle thousands of tons of fish. The fishermen haul the nets in as tight as they can and scoop the quota of fish they are allowed out with hoop nets slung from the mast. When they have their quota they simply let loose the ring net and hundreds of tons of dead fish sink to the bottom of the sea.

Cornish trawlermen complain that their nets are constantly being brought to a halt by running into mountains of stinking dead mackerel on the bottom of the ocean.

Thus do very few of the well-meant regulations of governments have the effect intended. They nearly always misfire. The Russian midwater trawlers are no longer allowed to search for mackerel inside the British fifty-mile limit. So what do the Russians do? They send a huge factory ship right into Milford Haven where she lies at anchor, and Scottish midwater trawlers sweep up the fish and pump them straight into the Russian ship. In Irish fishing ports hundreds of tons of prime fish are 'bought into intervention' by officials of the E.E.C., sprayed with blue dye so that they are unsaleable, and taken to sea and dumped. This is to 'maintain the price'.

It is thought by landsmen that the seas, being so vast, are inexhaustible. This is not so at all. Only the continental shelves are fecund with fish, and these extend only a few hundred miles from the shore.

The Japanese roam all the oceans of the planet seeking what they may devour. It is not that they are more greedy than the rest of us – simply more successful. They *know* their fleets are going to destroy the fish – and the intelligent and marvellous whales – to extinction and they seem not to care. The Japanese government has offered a bounty for every dolphin destroyed, simply because dolphins eat fish, and *every* fish belongs, as of divine right, to the Japanese. The Americans admit that *they* have killed five million dolphins incidentally in their netting of tuna: by mistake as it were.

I am sorry to go on so long about fisheries, but after all this planet is seven-tenths sea and all Life came from the waters. It is important.

I write not without experience of fishing and fisheries. Before the War I fished for over a year in southern African waters. As I had had some experience of the sea I started as mate of a forty-eight-foot fishing boat and ended as skipper. Our quarry was the snoek.

This was pre-Industrial – Revolution fishing. True we had an engine, but we fished with handlines. The snoek is a fine fighting fish, and about two feet long, in Australian waters called the barracuda. There were seven men aboard and the most we ever caught, in a day, was nineteen hundred. We headed, flecked, and salted these fish, stayed at sea about a month until our salt was finished, and then returned to port. There were six ships engaged in this fishery in South West African waters – ours was the smallest. If we had gone on till doomsday we would have made no impression whatever on the shoals of fish.

But the snoek feed on pilchard. After the war it was deemed better to catch the latter and leave the snoek alone. When I returned to Walvis Bay after the War there were forty big motor cutters, each operating huge ring nets, supplying three fishmeal factories. The shoals of pilchards – which in my time were miles and miles across and as thick as porridge – were dwindling rapidly. They are doomed to extinction. The shoals of anchovies and sardines off Chile are already all but extinct. This has pushed up dramatically the price of fishmeal. The seas are being swept dry to feed broiler chicken for 'finger-lickin'' goodness, and battery hens.

Nothing – nothing – can save animal life in the seas now, or at least the lives of every creature that could be of any possible use to Mankind – except perhaps a complete change of consciousness, and of the conscience of Mankind, a complete change in our attitude to the rest of the Universe, our attitude to the rest of Nature, which is what this book is about.

The great baleen whales of the Antarctic having been all but exterminated, *Homo extinctor* is turning his attention to their erstwhile food – the fields of krill, or small surface-feeding shrimps. These are to be swept up, too, into the maw of the fishmeal factories, to feed the spawning millions of Russia and

Japan. Must every living creature go down the gullets of Mankind? Is this what we have been put here for?

I have known intimately old smacksmen and driftermen – who got their bread on deep waters in the age of sail. I have to say that they were among the most *noble* men I have ever met. Their intelligence, bravery, toughness and hardiness set them far apart from other people. I will never forget old Sam Larner singing to us:

> Sailing over the Dogger Bank, wasn't it a treat?
> The wind a'blowing east-nor-east so we had to give her sheet
> You ought to see us rally – the wind a'blowin' free
> A passage from the Dogger Bank to Great Grimsbee!
>
> So watch her, Twigger, watch her, the proper joobajoo!
> Give her sheet and let her rip we're the boys to put her through
> You ought to see us rally, the wind a'blowin' free
> A'sailin' from the Dogger Bank to Great Grimsbee!

That was a song sung by a member of that proud race *Homo sapiens*. It is legitimate for Man to pit his wits against the denizens of the deep with wind and sail and oar and hempen net. These people had a proper love and respect for and understanding of the prey they were hunting just as did, no doubt, the fishermen of Galilee whom Jesus helped catch 'the miraculous draught of fishes'.

I compare Sam Larner in my mind with a member of that other, newer species, *H. extinctor*, standing in his heated wheelhouse, watching dials, while his mighty steel diesel ship encircles several miles' radius of sea with a net, sweeping up and destroying every living thing in it, adult fish, spawn, immature fish, leaving nothing behind but emptiness, death and corruption and completely obliterating a complex and beautiful system of living interrelationships built up over millions and millions of years. I cannot give you an example of any of his songs. *Homo extinctor* doesn't sing.

* Since this was written a few deep water shoals have begun to return to the North Sea.

CHAPTER NINE

Of the Technological Revolution

But when we in our viciousness grow hard, –
O misery on't – the wise gods seal our eyes;
In our own filth drop our clear judgements; make us
Adore our errors; laugh at's while we strut
To our confusion.
William Shakespeare, *Antony and Cleopatra.*

I WAS DRIVING IN a fast car along a tarred farm road in California; I was nearly hypnotised by mile after mile of rows of tomato plants. The rows were at right angles to the road and disappeared on both sides to the horizon. The land of that valley was perfectly flat. Possibly the only reason why I was not hypnotised was that every so often a row was missing – a complete blank.

'Did the seed drill bung up there?' I asked my host.

'No,' he said. 'The fertiliser drill did.'

And he went on to tell me that nothing – nothing – neither weed nor crop – would grow on that land any more without a direct application of artificial fertiliser: nitrate, phosphate and potash.

The land was sterile. Having once been some of the most fertile land on this planet it was now completely sterile. Nothing but tomatoes had been grown on it for thirty years now, not one ounce of dung or compost had been put on it, no crop residue had been ploughed in. (To plough in the tomato haulm would be to encourage disease in this monocultural situation, so the haulm was burnt.) Instead every element that the plants needed was provided every year in inorganic form, together with plenty of water. It is well known that heavy and constant applications of artificial nitrogen 'burn up' the organic material in the soil (what happens is that the nitrogen feeds and makes active the putrefactive bacteria), and the leaching of the irrigation water and hot Californian sun had done the rest. The soil was completely sterile.

'Why don't you keep some animals and put manure on the land?' I asked.

'And where would I get labour to feed the animals, and muck them out, and all the rest of it? And on this scale – twenty-five thousand acres – how many animals would I need? Ten thousand?'

'Why don't you grow some break crops?'

'What – and buy more machinery than I already have to harvest them? I'm gonna show you my latest tomato-picking machine. I've just gone into debt to the tune of eighty-five thousand bucks to buy it.'

He took me to a huge hangar and showed me the new tomato-picking machine. It was as big as a small ship. Beside it was another, nearly as huge, which he had bought the year before for sixty-five thousand dollars.

'Why did you buy another one after only a year?' I asked.

'Because the old one took twenty-five wetbacks to ride on it and sort the tomatoes. This one needs only five wetbacks, it's got an electronic eye. Wetbacks are now unionised and are demanding big wages.'

Wetbacks are Mexican labourers. They have wetted their backs in swimming across a river to get, illegally, into the United States.

'What will you do with the old machine?' I asked.

105

'Scrap. Nobody wants it. I'll have to pay somebody one day to take it away. Come – I wanna show you something.'

He took me into his private garden. It was worked by hand on the new deep bed system and looked marvellously fertile. Amongst other crops there were some fine tomatoes.

'What the hell do you grow tomatoes in your garden for?' I asked, thinking of those countless miles of stunted bushes outside.

'What – do you think I'd eat that rubbish myself?' he said. 'Those comercial tomatoes are damn near tasteless. And we spray them with so many poisons I wouldn't eat one for any money. All they taste of is chemicals.'

'Do you enjoy your way of life?' I asked him.

'Look – I'm just like most tomato growers – I'm caught in a rat trap. I owe my body and soul to the packers. I'm in debt over my ears. If I sold the whole damn place I would *still* be in debt. I will never be out of debt in my whole life. I *hate* the way I'm farming. I know it's wrong. My father tells me about his quarter-block back in Kansas where he farmed with horses, and no poisons, and no chemicals, and was healthy and happy and was never in debt in his life. Now it has come to this. I can *never* get out of it 'til I die.'

He may not have used exactly those words but that is the sense of what he said to me.

Who gains from this technological method of farming? The farmer? No way. The consumer? Eating tasteless poisoned rubbish? No way. The soil? No way. Life on this planet?

Well the shareholders of the canning company are presumably alive, although I suspect that if I met some of them I would find it hard to believe it. The shareholders in the chemical companies of course, *they* benefit. Or do they really benefit? They get rich of course. But does that get them any nearer the throne of God, to use a Hindu, Muslim and Christian figure of speech?

Who then – or what – does benefit?

106

This particular form of 'farming' may be the very apotheosis of technological agribusiness but do not suppose it is rare, and only found in a few places.

I was forced to leave my own beloved county, Suffolk in England, because I could not stand the same sort of development any more. I saw my country – that had been immortalised by John Constable and Gainsborough and was, when I was a child, perhaps the loveliest landscape on Earth – turned in a couple of decades to a huge, hedgeless, woodless, treeless, barley and wheat prairie. Most of the fine old moated farmhouses were sold to city businessmen for weekend homes, the farm labourers – those men who in my childhood had seemed to me to be heroes – were kicked out (no sorry – 'made redundant' – I must not forget the decencies) to make way for machines, machines and more machines, and a kind of brute force – big-machine and chemical force – took the place of good husbandry. I am not going to burden this book with masses of figures (although I could) but I will just produce one comparison which I think says it all.

In 1939 sixty units of nitrogen were used per acre per year on average in Great Britain.

In 1968 the figure was 749 units.

Sixty goes into 749 over twelve times. Has there therefore been a twelve-fold increase in the crop? There has not. A ton of sulphate of ammonia, incidentally, takes a ton of coal-equivalent to produce it (sulphate of ammonia is one of the commonest forms of artificial nitrogen). At present this power is coming from natural gas and oil, not coal. And when the natural gas and oil are finished? Who feeds us then?

But modern Western agribusiness is so hooked on artificial nitrogen that it would produce *nothing* without massive yearly inputs.

Anybody who has read this book so far is no doubt well aware of all the 'doom' literature that has come out in the last two decades. I am not going to rehearse it all here. I am

107

not with the practical results of the attitude to the rest of Nature by Technological Man but with the attitude itself.

Alex Faulkner tells us that the Americans landing on the moon were 'evidence in an age of cynicism and gloom that man can still do anything he wants to if he has the will and the money to spend'.

Anything?

This same apologist incidentally gives us his list of the wonders that the moon-shots bestowed on us, making life so infinitely richer and more rewarding for us poor earthlings who had to stay behind. These are: a new kind of heart pacemaker (for keeping alive people who really ought to be dead), an electric coffee percolator, a portable twin-element glass-ceramic cooking surface, a King Pin for cooking roasts, the Sams Survival Bag, space blankets for sporting activities, the digital thermometer, a pen which writes upside down, soap with an inbuilt magnet so that it sticks to a steel wall, a silent communications alarm network, a gutter and roof seal, a liquid cleaner, a graffiti and paint remover, a long-lasting torch, Pillsbury food sticks, and the Streamlite spotlight.

Wow! I really don't know which to dash for first!

For years and years I have concerned myself with the effect on human beings of our 'modern age', and compared these effects with the effects of former ages. I am now solely concerned though with the effect of this age on the whole of Nature, and on us only incidentally, in that we are part of Nature too.

I could fill this book a dozen times with a list of the abominations and atrocities that Technological Man has perpetrated on the rest of Nature. I am torn between wondering whether Technological Man worships himself, or only the people he calls 'scientists'. I think it may be the latter. Here is just a tiny selection of quotes from *one* issue of an American magazine called *Science Digest*.

The first scientist ever to induce cancer in animal cells by radiation has – at last – performed the same feat in human cells. It's something dozens of people have been trying to do for years.

(If you live a life of hard work in the open air you do not get cancer. The disease is almost unknown amongst peasant people who live like that. Cancer is a product of 'science'.)

An infusion of 0.00000005 of a gram [of a 'sleep inducing hormone'] taken from the cerebrospinal fluid of a sleep-deprived goat, will put a rabbit to sleep.

Hooray!

A whole new breed of food additives that may sidestep the old health hazards has been developed . . . Dynapol, a research firm in Palo Alto, California, has succeeded in making nonabsorbtive food additives. They have linked food additives to molecular chains that are too big to be absorbed through the wall of the gastro-intestinal tract.

But why have the bloody things at all?

If – or rather when – technology allows people to decide the sex of a child will most people choose male?

Note the incredible arrogance of that 'or rather when'. The journalist goes on to say that they will choose male and that there will then be far too many males and the human race will become unbalanced. Well then – *why do it?*

The eyeballs of blindfolded volunteers were illuminated from below by a powerful fibre-optic bundle held in the mouth, pointing upwards towards the roof. The subjects could see a

109

diffused glow of light, and when the light in the fibre-optic bundle was turned rapidly on and off . . . they could detect the change.

Well scientists, if you try turning the light in a fibre-optic bundle rapidly on and off in *my* mouth I warn you, here and now, that I shall bang you on the head. Hard.

> It's not science fiction. The technology is available for a cross-country tunnel and magnet-powered train that can make the New York to Los Angeles run in less than an hour.

And why the hell should anybody want to get from one polluted and dreary place to another polluted and dreary place in less than an hour? Or in any period of time whatever?

Yes – I think it is the Great God Scientist that *H. extinctor* worships – not just himself. Oh Great and Mighty Supermen in White Overalls and Spectacles – grant we beseech Thee a train that will take us from New York to Los Angeles in an hour. And find out for us how we blink!

Mankind has shown right down the ages that he must have a God. Witness that macabre spectacle in Red Square in Moscow, where people file, endlessly, past a pickled corpse. (What did they do with Stalin when he fell from grace? Dump the cadaver in the municipal incinerator? We shall never know.) Witness the French, at their most atheistic stage after the Revolution, building that gruesome building the Pantheon in which to deposit the ashes of the glorious dead. And witness now the awe and reverence which contemporary people show to the Scientist. I treasure the memory of a photograph of our present beloved prime minister, here in Britain, bowing down on her knees on top of the pile of a nuclear power station. She was ostensibly down on her benders to peer through a piece of glass at the deadly stuff below her: she was really down there to worship the true god of her religion. It is perhaps significant that his name is Pluto – the God of the Underworld, of Hell.

And what do we expect the Great God Science to give us if we pray and sacrifice to it assiduously enough? Why what it is giving us. Freedom from all real work (although not freedom from endless paper-shuffling), plenty of finger-lickin' chicken (the fact that the chickens spend their little lives in hell to provide it need not concern us), life at a constant temperature so that we never have to feel the heat or the cold, endless tumescence and detumescence (sex) without any responsi-bility, and the ability to travel from one dreary place to another dreary place at the speed of sound. What more do we want? Surely this is Heaven-on-Earth? Just as well, as we all know in our heart of hearts there is no other Heaven. And as we all get richer, due to endless economic 'growth', we can all have *flambé* dishes flaring away at our restaurant tables, flips to Corsica and flips to Peru (to find in both places exactly what we would expect to find in any other parts of the globe – same junk food, same 'pop' music, same 'art', same gadgets for 'enjoying ourselves'), two cars and a tupperware 'yacht' which we pull about behind one of them on a trailer, we can *all* have all these delights. The worship of the Golden Calf never brought the Babylonians anything like it. And we can have our colour television in every room including the jakes.

Of all Gods that Mankind has worshipped during his time on Earth Science is the only one that has come up with the goods. Consider the poor New Guinea savages. Stone-Age men, they have invented the 'Cargo' cult. They hack out, with enormous labour, airfields in the jungle. And by these, in wooden towers, they keep endless vigil, firm in their pathetic faith that one day an aeroplane will land there laden with all the goodies that their hearts desire. Alas – no flying machine comes. They wait in vain. Ah but *our* flying machines come! Our deities bring us the goodies! Trust in the Man with the White Coat and all things shall be added unto you!

Unfortunately the Man with the White Coat has tunnel vision. He is so specialised, to reach the dizzy height in his particular 'discipline' (he works within certain *parameters* you know) that he is completely imbecilic in any other subject. It is part of *his* religion that if a thing can be done it will be done. If one of these daisies can find a way to blow up the world he *will* blow up the world, have absolutely no doubt about that.

There is such a thing as true science of couse – the real honest search for the significant – the search that really gets us nearer to the throne of God (to use religious terminology again). We cannot blame Einstein for making possible the development of the atomic bomb and we can admire him when, after thousands and thousands of little children had been horribly mutilated and, if they lived, condemned to drag out the rest of their lives in pain and misery because of his discoveries, he said that if he had known this would happen he would have been a watchmaker.

Any sensitive watcher on the sidelines now must be absolutely appalled at the dizzy speed at which our world of Life is hurtling to destruction. *H. extinctor* is wiping out species after species of other forms of life in his mad scramble for more and more *growth*. Growth of what? Growth of the immortal soul and spirit of Mankind? Like hell. Growth of numbers of colour television sets.

But why *shouldn't* the poor have as many goodies as the rich? Why *shouldn't* every Russian and Chinese have a motor car and – ultimately – an aeroplane? I have got a motor car. And if anybody says they shouldn't because the resources of the planet are not sufficient for it the answer of the worshippers is: science will provide the resources. The oil is running out? Oh they'll find more. That'll run out too? Well then there's coal. Ah but somebody has got to go down there and *get* it! No no – the scientists will find a way of gassifying it underground.

And then there's the mighty Nuke! The stubborn refusal of both worshippers and scientists to admit that the Nuke is completely uneconomic, can never be economic, and is desperately dangerous, is simply a measure of their realisation that their whole jamboree cannot go on without it. The oil *is* coming to an end – in their hearts they have that bleak and terrible knowledge. Hooray! We must pray that this happens while there is still *some* non-human life left on the planet. For it is the oil that gives *H. extinctor* his seemingly limitless power. Nothing has ever existed – nothing ever will exist – which provides energy as nearly free as a liquid that comes bubbling out of the ground in vast quantities whenever anybody drills a hole in the right place. Nukes? They can *never* provide energy as cheaply as that. Nuclear generated electricity is the most expensive yet developed on this Earth, if you count in the cost of disposing of its wastes. Before the oil started getting scarce, oil-generated power was the cheapest. Oh what a mistake the Life Force made when it stashed away that black liquid underground.

I pray that nuclear power will not work out, not because it is dangerous and dirty and will give us disease and damage our posterity but because the power it will give us if it works will allow us to continue the destruction of our planet.

You doubt whether we are in fact destroying our planet? Consider the Amazon jungles which are being burnt down, in vast sweeps, by greedy men intent on making money from the ten years' growth of grass on the thin laterite soil left after the destruction. They know the soil will all erode away in ten or fifteen years. But ten years is enough to make a fortune – and what greedy man wants more than a fortune? And if *I* don't do it somebody else *will* is their cry. And if the government says I must not do it – I will bribe the government. Too easy. And if I refuse to bribe the government somebody else will.

A *true* scientist, Ernst Gorch, has found a way of turning rain forest into food producing land without burning the forest. He has worked out a method in the forests of Costa Rica. It consists of felling the forest trees, extracting the saleable

113

timber but letting the 'slash' (branches etc) lie and rot and planting a carefully chosen succession of food-bearing crops among the fallen timber. Instead of being dissipated by burning, the wood rots slowly and puts its nutrients back into the soil. A 'three-dimensional agriculture' (food-bearing trees with food-bearing crops planted under them) develops which could be sustainable for ever.

The big operators are doing all they can to stop him: they have not stopped short of trying to get him murdered. Why? Because, although the long-term profits of his method are far greater than burning, the short-term returns are less. The *estancia* owners don't want the government to be convinced of the rightness of his way and pass legislation to stop the wholesale burning that is going on now. After all – the wealthy *estancia* owners are not interested in long-term profits. They want profit *now* so they can live it up like the Arabs do. Why should they wait? Why should they wait a minute? And what does it matter that every time they set fire to another great tract of forest a whole ecosystem, built up over billions of years, is turned to dust and ashes? What does it matter if more and more Indians are forced to flee into the jungle where they die of starvation and disease?

Climatologists are worried that the destruction of the forests may starve our atmosphere of oxygen? Don't believe them say the ranchers – they are cranks and doomsters. The *true* Man in the White Coat never says anything that is going to interfere with the profits of the industrialists. After all – who pays him? He may be God – but he is only God if he comes up with the right findings. Witness the instant-obloquy that overtakes physicists who come out against the development of nuclear power.

Homo extinctor or *Tyranohomo rex*? Which is the more fitting title? Our species rages over the planet like a pestilence – like a great beast. Every other life form, if it could think, would feel in deadly peril of us. Where ever Western man goes (and increasingly Southern and Eastern Man too – they are quickly catching on) he spreads desolation and disaster. To think of the utter insensate cruelty of exploding 'nuclear devices' on Pacific islands – islands teeming with animal and vegetable life – islands supporting millions of species of living things! If men are ever born sane again they will view such memories with loathing and horror. Whatever happens in the future, if Man survives, for the rest of eternity he should hang his head in shame.

CHAPTER TEN

The Ultimate Arrogance

*When righteousness is weak and faints and unrighteousness exults in
pride, then my Spirit arises on earth.*
Bhagavad Gita 4:7. (Translated by Juan Mascaro)

AND SO WE HAVE come to it: the Ultimate Heresy – the
Ultimate Arrogance if you like – the belief that Man is no
longer a part of Nature at all.

We see men now, wherever we look, so blinded by
arrogance and the worship of Man as God that they are doing
things that no one but the insane would do. To pile up
megadeaths – to lash the land with poisons until the very
penguins of Antarctica are affected – to build nuclear power
stations that we know must lead to pollution and death – to
ransack the planet for more and more materials for the
hopeless task of trying to satisfy an insatiable greed – to
slaughter Leviathan for petfood – to destroy the forest
covering the Earth for quick profits even though we *know* that
this may lead to changes in the atmosphere which could prove
terminal for us . . . these acts are the acts of madmen – men
maddened by the belief that they are both omniscient and
omnipotent, that they are, indeed, God.

And no matter how he longs to – so long as Man holds to
this heresy he cannot stay his hand. *Homo extinctor* will go right
on to the bitter end, and destroy himself and take all Nature
with him, unless somehow we can give him a change of heart.

What then should we believe?

Well, as we have discussed before, you cannot believe something just because it is expedient to do so. Maybe if the world had been able to go on believing that the Earth was the centre of the Universe and Heaven above it, with a God sitting up there on a throne – a God who had made Mankind in His image (and not the other way round) then we would not have got to this pass. We would not have come to the Ultimate Heresy. We would not have invented the atomic bomb.

But Galileo looked through his telescope – *and the world had to believe the truth.* My own *feeling* is – just as Galileo's was – that you must hold to the truth even if to do so means destroying the world. But I also feel that if you hold strongly enough to the truth, and carry your search for it all the way, you will end up by not destroying the world. If we knew enough we would not *make* the atomic bomb.

Even if we know that if we hold a certain belief it will save us we cannot just *turn on* a belief. We either really do believe – or we don't.

I can only believe what my reason and my feelings tell me to be true. I tried in the first part of this book to show that *with reason alone* we must come to the conclusion that there is some tendency, or Force, which causes non-matter to become matter, matter to become living matter, etc. You and I must both know that this is true because it is obviously true – just as Galileo saw that it was obviously true when he looked through his telescope that the planets weren't stuck to crystal spheres. You exist. I know you do because you are reading this book. I exist because I am writing it. And both of us came from non-living matter – and, ultimately almost certainly, from the Void.

We also know, if we can just suppress our overwheening human arrogance while we think, that we came from Nature and are a part of Nature too. I don't believe many educated people nowadays would deny that we are mammals, primates, and members of the animal kingdom. Our reason tells us this – so do our feelings.

Therefore we are manifestations of the Life Force. And the Life Force has not evolved/created/produced us just for nothing – and it has not done it just for ourselves.

We are an experiment. The phenomenon of intelligence on this Earth is an experiment – by evolution – by Life – by the Life Force – by God – it doesn't really matter much what you call it. And the experiment succeeds or fails according to whether or not it serves the purpose of the Life Force. Like the Stegosaurus, either it fulfils the expectations of the Life Force or it does not.

A little blue tit has just hopped up the frame of my window, a few feet away from me, looking for flies. I imagine her saying to me: 'Yes – you are there for *my* benefit too. You are very intelligent and enormously powerful, but I must trust you because you have been put there not to be a tyrant and murderer but to be a true husbandman – you will not use your great power to destroy my nest and my children and my habitat. You will love and respect me.'

OH MAN THE HUSBANDMAN – Latin that!

How I would glory if that were to be our name! How much more beautiful that sounds in my ears than *Man the Wise* or *Man the Tyrant – Man the Destroyer*!

Nature has produced *brain* for her purpose and brain has gone mad. Brain in its arrogance has come to believe that *it* is the purpose – that the Nature which produced it is there for *its* benefit – that brain is the purpose of the Universe.

But it is not only that we humans are arrogant – that we worship ourselves. It is that our thinking brains are arrogant even within our own bodies!

This may be the root of our disease – that the reasoning parts of our brains feel separated from, and superior to, the rest of our bodies. Maybe we must start right there in our effort to cure our disease.

Western man has come to believe that only his brain is of any importance to him – the rest of his body is merely there to carry it about. Only his brain is *him*. Joseph the Bushman knew that every cell in his body was himself.

Consider ourselves, yet again, as what we are: aggregations of cells, each one a living being in itself. I am not asking anybody to pretend something that is not obviously true – we *know* that is true. Anybody can look down a microscope and see for himself. Nowhere in this book have I asked the reader, yet, to believe anything that reason alone does not tell him is the case.

Right then, we are aggregations of cells. The cells have formed themselves into specialised roles, to ensure the survival of the whole aggregation and thus their own individual survival too. Some cells form our spleen, some our left big toe, some our brain. *They are all of equal importance!* So long as a cell is still alive, and part of us, it is just as important to 'us' as any other cell. It is arrogant of the aggregate of cells that make up our brain to assume that 'they are the greatest' – that the rest of the body is there just for them.

Have you ever noticed that, when you have a really beautiful orgasm, it feels as if every particle of your body is shouting for joy? As you lie there, in the arms of your beloved, you experience an intense feeling that every single cell in you has shared in that explosive experience.

And every cell has of course. The cell that went forth from your body into the body of the beloved (assuming that you are a man) is the emissary – the representative – of them all. If that spermatozoon achieves its aim – the immortality of posterity – then it confers that immortality on every other cell in you. (If you are a woman read ovum for spermatozoon – sorry I'm a man, but it's just the same.)

The brain of overintellectualised Western Man – the 'Man in the White Coat' – has cut itself off from the rest of the body of which it is part. It is like the court of France when it had so far distanced itself from its subjects that that unfortunate queen said: "Let them eat cake."

The cells that form our brains may well be considered the court, or government, of the 'people' – the other cells in our body. But the true philosophy says: 'The king is the servant of his people.' I, as husbandman on sixty-two acres, may be king of the millions of living creatures that share these acres with me. I can kill, control, encourage, spare, cut down, cause to breed, prevent from doing so. But, if I wish to be a *husbandman* and not a tyrant, I must remember every moment that, being a king, I am also a servant. It is *all life* on my farm that I must consider and work for – not just arrogantly look upon all other life but me as there for my own selfish benefit. Look what happened to the Queen of France. Nature has a guillotine too.

And so the cells that form my brain – and the brain itself, considered as a single integrated object – must so consider the whole of my body. Every time I wonder what to believe – what to do – I should consult the whole of me – all those other living entities that make me what I am. I am convinced Joseph the Bushman did that. When I enjoy, every cell in my body shall enjoy. When some of them suffer I shall suffer too. We must stop our overactive, overarrogant brains from forgetting that they are our servants as well as our kings.

Maybe that is the state that the yogis are striving for. Last week I engaged in my own particular form of yoga. I walked for five days, twenty-five miles a day, over very rough country in the Welsh mountains. I forced my body almost to the limits of endurance – and I felt that every cell that makes up this assemblage I call me was glorying in being pushed to its limits – was glorying in the challenge of it and also in the transcendent beauty of those mountains. I felt once when I stood on top of the Rhinogs, and looked over the incredible blue of Cardigan Bay far away and far beneath me that every cell in my brain and body was glorying in that aesthetic experience, not just the part of my brain that receives the sight messages from my eyes. My eyes and the sight-receiving parts of my brain are not just there for their own enjoyment any more than the human species is on this planet for its enjoyment alone.

We do not *have* to postulate a soul. I ask nobody to believe such a thing any more than I ask anyone to believe in God. I ask you though to believe in a Life Force because your reason alone, if you use it well, must tell you that there has got to be a Life Force otherwise you wouldn't be here.

I believe in the soul. But this is a special kind of belief – it is *not* the kind of belief that you can come to by using reason alone and therefore *I do not ask anybody to share it with me*. Every person either does, or does not, come to that sort of belief by her or himself. And it is only when you learn to think *and feel* as a whole organism – every cell in your body sharing in the effort – that you can come to such conclusions. When Carlyle cried out to Nature, 'Art thou not the living garment of God?', he was expressing the fact that he had, through hard travail, torn away from the whole spirit of his age and come up with an idea that was the work of more than just his mind: his brain alone.

What then must we believe? If the human race is not to suffer the fate of Marie Antoinette we must believe that there is a Life Force, that it has developed us to further its own purposes and that we must do so. That is all. We are here to further the purposes of the Life Force. We have been evolved for just that. If we fail to do it Life will terminate the experiment. Every time a man orders the burning of another million acres of the Amazon jungle he is committing the deadly sin – the sin for which there can be no forgiveness. There is no old man with a beard up there who is going to strike him with a bolt of lightning. He will get exactly the same retribution that the nutcase would get who tried to cut his body off because only his brain was important to him. When a politician orders the explosion of another 'nuclear device' he

121

is committing the deadly sin. If there is a Hell he will be in it, for he is going grossly against the real needs and interests of the Life Force.

I believe a new consciousness is spreading over the world. It comes in many forms but it always says the same thing – much what I have already been trying to say in this book. If this consciousness prevails quickly enough then maybe there is hope for the present creation, or evolution, for Life on this planet. The time is desperately short. There are now a million megadeaths, poised, aimed, programmed, primed and ready, to be launched screaming across this pathetic planet at the whim of some elected fool. *Only* a completely new consciousness, spreading as quickly as a forest fire throughout the whole human world, can save us – and when I say *us* – I mean *us* – all terrestrial life: I mean the blue tit at my window too.

This new consciousness – this new religion if you like (a religion does not necessarily have to encompass the supernatural or the superstitious) – must purge its adherents completely and finally of the blasphemous illusion that Mankind is in any way apart from Nature or in any way here for himself alone.

I see it being born – I see it spreading. In nearly every country now for example is an 'organic movement' – a movement of people dedicated to finding a way of husbanding soil, crops and stock, and all wild living creatures, in a way that is not too tyrannical and destructive. *H. extinctor* endeavours to destroy every living thing, vegetable or animal, on his land that is not of direct economic benefit to him. Thus a wheat agribusinessman burns his straw after harvest – hoping to kill as many wild things with the fire as he can. He eliminates every possible hidey-hole for wildlife in the form of hedges, woods, heathland, wild places, and douses his crop as it grows over and over again with deadly poisons – herbicides – insecticides – fungicides – bacteriocides, viricides. I cannot call him a farmer, that is an honourable title: I call him a wager of war – a chemical warfare expert of the most ruthless and destructive kind.

The new type of farmer works quite otherwise. He understands the wholeness of all Life – and works with the Life Force, not against it. Far from trying to destroy all life in his soil, his constant endeavour is to *increase* it. He piles organic matter into his soil with the very object of encouraging the bacterial and fungal life that lives therein. He glories in the diversity of vegetable and animal life in and on his soil.

Of course he exercises control over Nature. He knows that in his role, he is Man the Husbandman. He keeps fair play. He sees that his own family gets fed of course – it is part of Nature too. But he does not ruthlessly poison or kill every living thing that is not of immediate benefit to him.

I glory every time I hear or read of yet another country in which an organic organisation has started up! I had a letter just yesterday from a Japanese one. Maybe the whales and dolphins will be saved after all.

Then there are groups all over the world, and growing quickly, striving to protect this or that aspect of Nature from the despoilers. A cosmic battle has been joined – like the Battle of Kurukshetra, the story of which is told in the Mahabharata. It is a battle between good and evil. Maybe it is a battle that, in cosmic terms, can never finally be won. I don't know. Maybe, even in times of apparent peace, some Childe Harold has to ride up to the Dark Tower and put his slughorn to his lips and blow a blast of defiance – and a blast of affirmation that Life is still there, and ready and willing to defend itself against the forces of darkness and of death.

CHAPTER ELEVEN

Getting Our Heads Straight

Not by refraining from action does man obtain freedom from evil. Not by mere renunciation does he attain supreme perfection. Action is greater than inaction: perform therefore thy task in life. Even the life of the body could not be if there were no action.
Bhagavad Gita 3: 4,8. (Translated by Juan Mascaro)

WHEN YOU COME FINALLY to accept the belief that *Man is part of Nature* you have completely to overhaul every one of your previous ideas about what it is right to do.

Things that seemed quite right before, now seem wrong. Things that seemed wrong seem right. At the advanced age of – what is it? – you must re-examine every one of your beliefs.

Well anything is better than getting in a rut.

But of this I am sure: we will get nothing right unless we can get our own spiritual values right. For nothing really has any significance for us any more, and so we just throw ourselves into the nearest game, and that is nearly always the game of scrabbling for money or the other (and related) game of scrabbling for power.

We belong to the generation that believes in nothing – and nothing has any real value or significance to us. Gai Eaton, in his book *King of the Castle* that I would love to quote *in toto* here, says:

> Remove from any object its sacred or symbolic aspects, tossing it into the flux of purely quantitative phenomena, and value dissolves like flesh from bones in a vat of acid.

124

My parents belonged to the *soi disant* 'enlightened' generation which had its heyday in the so-called 'roaring twenties'. I remember the 'roaring twenties' and they didn't roar at all – they expressed themselves in a series of high-pitched silly squeakings. They should be named – and I hereby name them – the Silly Twenties. This was the first truly godless decade and if a decade can be judged by its works it was the most worthless decade that Mankind has so far been through.

My parents' contemporaries were not agnostics – they were atheists (although some of them never admitted it). They did not believe in God at all. They attached nothing but a quantitative significance to anything. They spent their lives in an unrelenting search for pleasure, for pleasure was the only thing that could mean anything to them. The search for money had to come first of course, for you cannot have the sort of pleasure they were searching for without it. They found money and they found pleasure, of some low sort, but they did not look very pretty when they died. Then they learnt what Carlyle meant when he wrote 'a charnel house with spectres'. *They* certainly did not believe they belonged to Nature – they were not aware of the rest of Nature at all, except as something you saw flashing past through the vita glass windows of your chauffeur-driven motor car. (The vita glass was supposed to let the ultra violet rays through – didn't you know?)

Our present age is trying to discover God again. The great majority of us believe we have found Him. We have only to look into the mirror haven't we? Or at the nearest Man in a White Coat? A minority – the bearded and long-haired minority – are trying everything, from astrology to ley lines to Hare Krishna. Perhaps they are on a better scent. Perhaps, though, they would do better, if they are Westerners, to re-examine their own religious tradition and see if this could not be made to live again.

In former ages most people didn't have to search for God: they simply knew He was there. They may have had all sorts of things to worry about in those days. Some were hungry (but few so hungry as the people starving in the expanding deserts of the Sahel now), some were oppressed (but none more oppressed than the tribal Indians of the shrinking Amazon rain forests), some were humiliated (but none more humiliated than the modern junior executive just lapped in the office rat-race). But they all *knew* there was a God, they were all *sure* of an afterlife, and the artefacts they left behind them were almost without exception beautiful. And they did not bear heavily on the rest of Nature at all, while our merry atheistical generation is hell-bent on destroying Her.

I now have a confession to make which will invalidate nearly everything I have written in this book in the eyes of many of its readers. I believe in God. I am not asking *anybody* else to share my strange belief. Yes – I even pray! I don't grovel on my knees like Maggie Thatcher on top of the atom pile – I stand, out of doors, with my head high, and fling my arms out wide and open to embrace, ritually, all the matter of the Universe, animate and inanimate. I do also, humbly and contritely, fall to my knees before the Blessed Sacrament but this is my own affair and nothing to do with anybody else.

I do ask you to share my belief in the Life Force, or the Tendency that has made Life, because I believe I have made out a rational case for this, but I do not even want you to share my belief in God. The reason is that every human being must come to the realisation of God by himself. There is little that his conscious mind can do to help him. He must do it with his whole being – every cell of him. I believe there have been revelations in times gone by. Some of the writers of the Bible, Jesus himself, Gautama, some Hindu sages – even many seers and prophets much nearer our own day – have actually been 'messengers' – they have been granted superhuman insights that are not granted the rest of us. Happy the people who followed them and still believed their messages. Their lives were simple and satisfying. Unhappy the people like our own generation who have forgotten what these messages were and must try desperately to unravel the whole thing out again for themselves. We are assuredly the do-it-yourself generation: we even have to reinvent God!

I believe, with Gai Eaton whom I must mention again, that Man is the Viceroy of God among the living things on this planet. It is an awe-inspiring responsibility. And I believe that, like many another viceroy of a human king, Man is getting above his station. He is beginning to believe he is the King himself. He is no longer trying to carry out the wishes of his sovereign: he is becoming a tyrant in his own right. We all know what happens to viceroys who try to set up thrones for themselves – if their masters are powerful enough. Look what happened to Mark Antony! And our Master is very powerful, make no doubt about that.

I know you probably want to know what we must *do* and here I'm on about what we must believe. But you see there is no hope whatever of us doing the right things unless we get our heads straight first. Unless we can again invest the living things around us with *significance* – with a more than quantitative and secular significance – we will not deal rightly with them whatever we do. There is a larch tree growing just by my gate. It is growing crooked and will never make good timber and it is hampering the growth of a magnificent beech. Furthermore it spoils my view. It has just as much right to live as I have but I shall cut it down as I have cut down many hundreds of trees in my life (ah but I have planted thousands more). But when I cut it down I shall do it with love and respect. You can't cut down something that you love and respect? Oh yes you can. When I get too old to be any more use I hope fervently that somebody who loves and respects me will cut me down. I will cut that old tree down and when I do so I will say 'Sorry sister' and I truly believe the tree – or something

– will hear me and will forgive me in its soul. The cattle ranchers who put matches to the tinder-dry Amazon forests in the dry season in the hope of making a quick buck do not do so with love and respect. I believe there has got to be some sort of hell and I believe those people have got to be in it. Or should I say, as somebody else did once: 'Forgive them for they know not what they do!' Well it's up to us to make damn clear to them right quick the import of what they do.

But if I had no feeling in my soul of the sanctity of Life – of all Life – and of all matter in fact – I would have no feeling for the old larch tree. And the reason why I do feel the sanctity of the larch tree is that I know that, as Carlyle put it, it is part of the living garment of God! Don't ask me how I know this – and I do not ask you to join me in the knowledge. It would be perfectly pointless for me to do so because this is a knowledge that you cannot arrive at with your conscious mind. I probably arrived at it one night when I was driving in a *tonga* (a horse-drawn hackney carriage) under the splendid stars of India, pissed out of my mind, with the tonga-wallah equally pissed (we had been drinking seven-year-old arak together) over a dam across the River Indus. The drunken tonga-wallah was singing some wild hymn and suddenly he stopped and turned to me and (neglecting the horse which was completely sober) flung his arms out and shouted 'There is a God!' and we both shouted it out together in our different languages, but we both understood exactly what the other meant!

There is no hope whatever of us making beautiful things again, composing fine music, writing (or saying) fine poetry, building great buildings, until we resume, consciously and proudly, our viceregal functions.

I know I have no hope whatever of persuading any reader, through his conscious mind alone, to believe in any God. But I have every hope, if he will only use his conscious mind conscientiously enough, to persuade him he is part of Nature (is he not a vertebrate, a mammal, a primate, descended from other forms of life, and therefore *related* to all other, non-human forms of life? If you don't believe in God you've just got to believe in that); that Nature has evolved him for her own purposes (not his alone); and that therefore he must – or at any rate should – join me in striving to save what little is left of Nature-not-Man on this planet. I could ask him to do this anyway for selfish reasons alone (if the rest of Nature goes it will bring man down with it), but I consider this unworthy.

What then can we do?

The first thing is to learn the lesson of the Baghavad Gita and engage in action not because we think we will succeed but because we think it is right. You can say, 'There is no point in my refusing to buy the produce of the whaling industry because I am only one among five hundred billion people and my abstention can have no bearing whatever on the result', and you will, in mathematical terms, be completely right. You must abstain from buying such goods because it is right to abstain – *for no other reason.* This may, to a purely practical person, seem stupid and unreasoning. It is *not* stupid and unreasoning because it is the only motivation for action that will work. If we abstain from buying whale products because we think our miniscule abstention will have the slightest effect on the issue we are wrong. It won't. But if we abstain because *we know it is right to abstain* – because we know that modern whaling is an evil thing and that we are condoning evil to be associated with it – then our abstention *will* effect the final issue. In the end our condemnation of evil will spread and, together with that of a billion others, will work.

The only way in which you or I can affect the issue of whether Life survives on this planet or not is to consider every action we do, or consciously abstain from, after asking this question: 'What effect will this action or abstention have on the rest of Life on this planet? Will it be pleasing or displeasing to the Life Force?' According to the Law of Gravity if you lift your little finger you move the furthest stars. At least I have never heard any amendment to the Law of Gravity which says there is any distance limit to the operation of gravity – correct me if I am wrong oh Great Man in the White Coat! – but of course the M.I.T.W.C. doesn't believe in anything he can't measure. If one of us makes the smallest action which is pro-Life for the right motive (i.e. because he knows that it is right) the consequences of that action reach out into the Universe like the ripples from a stone thrown into a pond.

The best-willed of us compromise incessantly. I have a Russian car which I know was made by slave labour in some enormous and anti-Life factory in the Urals, from steel torn from the bosom of the living Earth, driven with petrol that derives from wells over which there will probably soon be a nuclear holocaust. I switch on the electric light knowing that part of it derives from poisoning and polluting nuclear power stations (how I can oppose the opening of uranium mines in Donegal when I happily use nuclear-produced electricity I find it only *too easy* to understand – I am a hypocrite). You probably do all these things too. If you go into one of those disgusting places which serve American-style hamburgers you are most certainly helping to finance the South American jungle-burners. Your hamburger should taste of napalm – and the blood of murdered Indian tribes. We do, every one of us, compromise and compromise and it seems almost impossible not to do so. I say 'With my Russian car I can get around quickly and cheaply and try to persuade people not to do things which are anti-Life.' But if I listened to that other injunction from the same old *Baghavad Gita* which says 'The ends never justify the means' I would not do this. All I can do is to say: 'Don't do what I do – do what I say!' and really what can be more feeble than that?

It has been said that we of this generation are not to be judged so harshly or exigently as people of former generations. Our problems are too convoluted – too obscured and involved. I interpret this as meaning we should not judge

130

ourselves as harshly as the people did in former, simpler, ages. We have been led slowly and almost imperceptibly into closer and closer involvement with 'The Thing', as old Cobbett called it – the great worldwide conspiracy to cheat and despoil Mother Nature for our own supposed benefit. We are like junkies – we are completely hooked. We try to kick the habit suddenly and find the break too violent. Therefore we compromise and compromise.

Maybe we have *got* to compromise if we are going to achieve anything at all.

Every single judgement that we have to make is hard – hard. Nothing is simple. And if you start to judge the rightness of actions according to whether they are 'pleasing' or 'displeasing' to the Life Force it is still hard.

War is bad? Well when the Israelis bombed the Iraqi nuclear power station they may have been saving the world. The best thing that could happen now is that the Iraqis should return the compliment and bomb theirs.

Child mortality is bad? There is nothing in the world more heart-wringing than to see a mother mourning over a dead child. And do you think the shrinking remnant of the wild animals of Africa mourn when they see a dead human child? An African farmer might just as well mourn when he sees a dead locust. It is the *live* locusts he mourns about.

Death is bad? Are we to stop it then? If the Men in the White Coats *could* they would confer on us all physical immortality. Would this, indeed, be pleasing to the Life Force? Is it pleasing to it when 'life' is kept in some would-be cadaver long after it should have died? Is it good for me to take over a piece of wasteland behind my house and turn it into a garden or not? Wasteland is becoming very scarce on this planet and, anyway, what right have we got to designate a piece of natural country, teeming with living things, as *waste*? And yet what could be more pleasing to the Life Force than an harmonious garden, bursting with fertility, and possibly nurturing even more

131

species of living things than the original wild place? And furthermore feeding me. How am I going to answer this question?

Fortunately I do not have to answer it alone.

When I wrestle with such problems with my conscious mind I have the feeling, sometimes, that I am indeed stuck in a quagmire. But if I allow my whole being to participate – and if I allow the whole of the natural world *of which I am a part* speak through my being and my brain – then I come up with answers and I think that, very often, they are the right ones. This is what Christians used to call 'listening to the Voice of God'.

CHAPTER TWELVE

What, Then, Are We to Do?

Set thy heart upon thy work, but never on its reward. Work not for a reward; but never cease to do thy work. Do thy work in the peace of Yoga and, free from selfish desires, be not moved in success or in failure.
Bhagavad Gita 2:47,9 (Translated by Juan Mascaro).

I NOW PROPOSE, WITHOUT making any more bones about it, to examine various issues in the light of this question: what is the best course to follow for all of Nature – including ourselves?

Obviously we must start with agriculture, for this has been the basis of our existence since Neolithic times at least, and is likely to go on being so if we are to survive at all.

Even agricultural 'experts' can see now (as people like me could fifty years ago) that the present system of agriculture in the West is unsustainable. It depends *entirely* on oil and gas-derived inputs. After the great agricultural boom since the Second World War there is now an agricultural depression, and an industry completely hooked on sophisticated machinery and huge chemical inputs is finding it very hard to carry on. Nearly every decision farmers have taken during the last forty years has been influenced more than anything else by the cost of labour. The high cost of labour has forced farm amalgamations until the size of farms has doubled and doubled again and again. It has forced on heavy mechanisation, indebtedness to the banks, introduction of

133

monocultural systems, the divorcing of the animals from the land (with consequent utter dependence on chemical fertilisers) and the dog-chasing-its-tail syndrome of stronger and stronger poisons chasing endlessly more and more resistant pests and diseases.

Even if the oil were *not* going to run out the thing would be unsustainable. Agribusiness seems to have managed to break the laws of Nature so far – but *with brute force*. Enormous mechanical power aided by massive applications of more and more sophisticated poisons has enabled men to farm – and to make fortunes – without obeying the rules of good husbandry at all. The rules of good husbandry are:

1. You must work with Nature and not against Her.
2. Nature is diverse and so you must practise diversity.
3. The animal and the plant kingdoms are complementary and neither must be ignored.
4. You must labour to increase the organic content of your soil.
5. Excessive damage from pests and diseases is a sign of bad husbandry and you must not kill for the sake of killing.

I don't know whether these laws have been formulated before, but these were the rules that were taught to me by that good old farmer, Mr. Catt of Feering, Essex, when I learnt farming from him sixty years ago.

All these laws are being broken, continuously, by today's agribusinessmen. It's easy to condemn the latter for it – but they can't help it! The price of labour makes it impossible for them to employ more than skeleton staffs, the price of capital and of land makes it necessary for them constantly to take on bigger enterprises, lack of labour forces them to adopt monoculture and mechanise and chemicalise and successive governments stand by and shout hooray! Fewer people on the land means more in the factories – and the *factories* are where the money comes from after all!

And meanwhile the non-farming consumer stands by and sees his country becoming a potential desert, his food falling in quality and variety, and with the growing realisation that if the Arabs decided to cut off the oil he would very quickly starve.

Well, from the point of view of Nature-not-Man the result of all this has been one of steadily increasing degradation and impoverishment. If you don't believe this go and look at John Constable's painting *The Cornfield* (the one with the boy lying down on his tummy drinking from a stream) and go to the Stour Valley and try to find the viewpoint of the artist now. I did. The stream the boy was drinking from is piped, so all the living things that lived in it don't exist. The great trees that stood to the left of the boy have all been cut down and their stumps bulldozed out. The place when I saw it was just one large flat barley field, but you could hardly see it for overhead cables and wires. The field is sprayed regularly and frequently with poisons which are aimed to destroy every living thing except barley. What would Constable have made of that? What would he have had to paint?

Make no doubt of it – the land when I saw it was growing more corn per acre than it was when Constable painted *The Cornfield*. But also make no doubt of it – the barley that I saw is the produce of the oil wells, not the soil. The wheat that Constable painted was grown without an ounce of artificial fertiliser whatever – and not a single spray. It was entirely the product of the soil, it had to be because there was nothing else.

As for the aesthetic difference between the scene Constable painted and the one I saw, well it's pointless even to talk about it: there is just absolutely nothing to be said about it. 'He that hath eyes to see let him see.'

I have a friend who, with his brother, farms twelve hundred acres in Sussex. These two do their best to farm well, and are by no means oblivious to the rules of good husbandry. They milk two large herds of Ayrshires, they have a huge herd of breeding sows (kept indoors under conditions which certainly would not please me – nor, I should think, do they please the sows), they keep sheep up on the downs, so that they are not depriving the land of all animal manure. True they need much more of it than they have got: twelve hundred acres is an *enormous* piece of land. They employ a dozen people: a tenth of the number this farm employed in their grandfather's day. The people are well paid, well fed, and well housed. One of them complained to me that the only thing about his work was that he was desperately lonely, but that is a complaint common to all modern farm labourers. These farmers have a film made by their father, in the 1920s, about the farm activities, and the one thing that the present farm workers said when they saw this film was: 'How nice it must have been always to be working in company – those people were never lonely!'

But the loneliness of farm workers only has to do with Man – not the whole of Nature. It has to do with Nature only in so far as Man is a part of it. It is the effect of this kind of farming on Nature-not-Man that I find disturbing. And I say again – these two brothers are enlightened men and try to farm in the best way they can.

But to *pay* a dozen people they are forced to make a vast amount of money. To get good people they pay well above the odds and, with insurance and perks and all the rest of it they certainly get no change out of £200 a week per worker. *That makes £2,400 per week!* There is only one way they can possibly generate this sort of money and that is by growing enormous crops on their twelve hundred acres. To do this by organic methods alone would mean employing vastly more people! Then the wage bill would be even higher and they would need to grow even bigger crops. Thus they *cannot* change to organic agriculture even though they want to. They *have* to grow three tons of wheat per acre and this they can only do by lashing their land with petrochemicals. One of the brothers at least feels in his bones that these are not going to go on for ever. He knows his land could grow practically nothing without them though, unless it were regenerated by organic methods. He asked me once what I would do if I were him and I answered: 'Cut the land up and divide it up amongst a hundred people who could farm it intensively and organically.' He answered, and with perfect rightness, that if he did that the planning laws would not allow these people to build houses.

Of course his problem *will solve itself* when the oil and gas run out. But I felt sad that I could offer no idea for a course of action that could be followed *now* – for surely it is better for men to take the right course because they know it is right and not wait to be forced along it by external forces.

It will be argued for the apologists of agribusiness that you could not grow three tons of wheat to the acre by organic methods alone. It is true that there are organic techniques being worked out in California and other places for growing an extraordinary amount of food on a small area of land but these are gardening techniques not farming ones. It is also true that wheat can perfectly easily be grown by these techniques, but with an enormous amount of labour. But I am quite willing to concede that, with any ordinary agricultural practice, you are not likely to achieve three tons of wheat to the acre by organic methods alone. With inorganic methods though – including the use of a vast number of poisonous sprays – you can.

Right then, says the agribusiness apologist – the present population of the planet being what it is people would starve if we had to abandon agribusiness.

Now to counter this statement from the point of view of Nature-as-a-whole one must say *'Then there are too many people.'* It is not right that any species should get so numerous as obviously to be out of balance. When rabbits became out of balance before myxomatosis struck them they were a bloody nuisance to everything else. They prevented natural regeneration of woodland completely. They caused a most serious degradation of grassland. Rabbit-infested land was poisoned land and looked it. Why did they get out of balance? Because arrogant men hunted down and destroyed nearly all their predators. The only engine used on a widespread scale by Man to control the rabbit was the gin trap. The gin trap actually *increased* the number of rabbits. Why? Because placed as it was it destroyed all the rabbits' predators. Foxes, weasels and stoats all fell to the gin trap, for they all hung about outside rabbit burrows, or tried to get in, and were practically exterminated. The game-preserving landlords, with their gamekeepers, did the rest. Thus, by artificial means, a species was allowed to get out of balance. Myxomatosis was a cruel and disgusting thing but it redressed this balance: now I can go out and plant a tree, without putting a rabbit-proof fence around it, with some hope of the tree prospering.

It is difficult not to draw a parallel between rabbits and men.

If the land of this planet has to be flogged with poisons to produce enough food to feed humans then there are too many humans.

I realise that what I have just written will damn me completely in the eyes of every right – (and left) – thinking liberal, humanist, humanitarian, Christian, pagan, and everybody else. But remember I am examining the question from a totally new standpoint: *not* from the standpoint of Man but from the standpoint of *all* Life on this planet (or in the Universe).

And, paradoxically, the health of each species seems to be bound up with the health of all. Man cannot divorce himself from the rest of Nature and suppose that he can proliferate indefinitely at the expense of every other living thing. It just ain't going to work.

Witness India. There are just far far far too many Indians. Far from indicating that the species Man is very successful in India it indicates the opposite. If Indian Man does not take care he will be on the way out. For the *soil* of India is being savagely eroded and the fertility of the rest reduced. Its forests are being cut down and not replanted. The relentless pressure of its ever-increasing population is endangering the survival of Life itself on the subcontinent. The overpopulation is due to two things; improved health services and past foreign food aid. Both are enemies of the true interests of all Life in India – including the life of Man.

The social pressure to breed many children evolved in India when infant mortality was very high. Now Indian child mortality has been drastically reduced these social pressures are still there and Indians go on breeding as hard as ever they can. The increasing population due to this can only be kept alive by two means: increased food production in India and foreign food imports. Neither is indefinitely sustainable, and what is going to happen when they fail? I was in Calcutta during the 1943 Bengal famine and I know.

And India is an extreme example of what is happening all over the world. *Homo extinctor* is pressing harder and harder on all other forms of Life. Possibly some Men in the White Coats imagine a world with no non-human Life in it, or at least a very little and that all closely controlled by – guess who? A scenario could easily be dreamed up in which all the habitable parts of the planet are human-occupied suburbs – something between Wimbledon and Palo Alto – with a few specimens of as many species of animals and vegetable as can be saved from the present holocaust (hundreds of species are becoming *extinct* every year nowadays) kept safely in zoos or game parks, power and heat for the ever-rising needs of humanity provided by tens of thousands of nuclear power stations (all manned by infallible Men in White Coats of course), food provided by hydroponics on a shrinking acreage of unbuilt-over land, human population a thousand billion and rising exponentially – and everything in the garden absolutely beautiful. Not *quite* as we imagine the Garden of Eden but nevertheless imaginable.

Of course the age we live in is the quantitative age. Quantity – numbers – mean everything. The M.I.T.W.C. can deal with no other factor. Quantitative science can find everything out about anything *except what it really is*. When the *Bhagavad Gita* was written down first there were probably less than a million people in the whole of India. Now there are lots more. Has the quality of Life improved? Or is it better to have five hundred million unhappy people than a million happy ones?

I realise I am skating on very thin ice here and many people are already reaching for their horse-whips. What – the man is actually suggesting that we should kill people off – or allow babies to die – just so that *he* can have plenty of room? Well no it's not like that. I am merely going through the exercise of trying to consider a question from the point of view of Nature-not-Man. Thinking as a *Man* I know I would give my own life to stop *any* baby from dying. But in the above piece of reasoning I am not thinking as a Man but as a representative of the whole of Nature, because I have accepted the hypothesis that Man is part of Nature and not apart from Her. And if I have to sit in a judgement chair and pass judgement on some species which has got out of control and is upsetting and distorting the balance of Nature to the distress of every other living thing – then I have to be an impartial judge and condemn that species if I find it guilty, even if it is my own. Fortunately I am not any sort of a judge and as I explained in the last chapter I know there is a Judge who judges of such matters. Call Her Mother Nature if you like and I shall be content. Or call her The One.

So I do not have to pass sentence. But sentence will be passed. The Men in the White Coats may get stay of execution but then they will appeal in vain. The following is a paragraph from a publication of the Environment Liaison Centre in Nairobi. The figures it presents are derived from a report of UNEP (The United Nations Environment Programme).

Over the last decade, the Earth's soils underwent severe degradation; up to 70,000 square kilometres are estimated to have gone out of production, mainly because of soil erosion, salinity and nutrient leaching. The misuse of agro-chemicals complicated the effort to increase food production and keep farmworkers free of contamination.

Some of the less short-sighted Men in White Coats can see that the soils of the Earth are doomed with our present methods of farming but they think this does not matter because we can go over to producing food by hydroponics – that is soilless culture: the plants are held up on frameworks and provided with all the nutrients they need by water carrying the nutrients in solution. Only the people with tunnel vision can believe that this is going to sustain anything like the world's existing population. In the first place all plants depend on *fixed* nitrogen – nitrogen that is in a compound combined with oxygen. This is very unstable stuff and the nitrogen is always trying to get free again, in which condition it is of no use whatever to plants. Now Life has learnt to fix nitrogen on a massive scale. Every ounce of good soil is teeming with nitrogen-fixing bacteria. Man-without-the-rest-of-Nature can only fix nitrogen with colossal expenditure of power (he does it by producing an electric spark). If we eliminate all the bacterial fixation of nitrogen (as we do when we lose our soil) the demand for artificially fixed nitrogen will rise to enormous heights: we would require far more power to make it than this little planet could ever provide.

In spite of all the efforts of the Men in the White Coats famine is spreading on this planet faster than it has ever spread before.

But, from the point of view of Nature-not-Man it is not spreading fast enough! It is not spreading fast enough to save the Sahel – the pastoral lands surrounding the Sahara – from desertification. It is not spreading fast enough to save the richest biomass in the world: the rain forests of Central and South America, and of Sri Lanka and Indonesia, from the fires of Man's greed. It is not spreading fast enough to save the alluvial plains of India from galloping erosion and salination. (I have seen miles and miles of formerly fertile country in the Indus Valley as white as snow with salt and abandoned for cultivation: the result of ill-considered giant irrigation schemes – and this story can be repeated wherever huge-scale irrigation systems have been established.) It is not spreading fast enough to save the Life in the Seas.

Half the world is now hooked on North American wheat and maize. When *they* fail what happens then? When I flew, a few years ago, from Heathrow to California, as I mentioned before, I looked down at the chequer-board that is the North American Great Plains. The cancers of soil erosion were to be seen everywhere. The pattern of soil erosion was the only pattern that cut across the monotony of mile-wide squares that North America has become.

I am not romancing or bragging when I say that I would die to save any child in the world. All Life is sacred and young Life is the most sacred of all because it has longer to go. I would barter my life to save the life of anyone in the world younger than I am. (I would not move a finger to save an old person from a natural death.) But I still think there are too many people on this planet for the good of themselves – or any other forms of Life. If certain of the Hindus are right and every one of us has a soul and that soul derives from the beginning of time and each soul that is disembodied is waiting in some limbo to be born – then I think we are in too much of a hurry to achieve a high throughput of souls. Let 'em wait a few centuries longer: as my old friend Satish Kumar says, 'When God made Time He made plenty of it.'

So how do we reduce the number of people? Well fortunately we don't have to do it. There are some things we can leave to greater powers than our own. But we *could*, as the

Indians are trying to do and the Chinese are succeeding in doing, stop having so many babies.

I am not likely to forget what I saw of the Bengal Famine in 1943. I was on leave from the army in Burma (where I had become quite used to seeing corpses – indeed, making them) and I put up at the United Services Club on Chowringee. Chowringee is the posh street – like Regent's Street perhaps, or Piccadilly. The U.S.C. was a good old-fashioned club, with big rooms, electric fans, polite servants, very good food and plenty of it.

The servants pulled the dead and dying away from the actual doors of the club. Out on the pavement you stepped over them. Bullock carts, operated by the municipality, trundled along collecting the dead. There was no smell. I pushed a rupee into the hand of a living skeleton of a man. His wife lay dead beside him but the baby, clinging to the corpse, was still alive. The man looked at the rupee and let it drop on the pavement. His eyes didn't even thank me. What good was a rupee to him?

I do not want to see another famine. I do not want there to *be* any more famines. This particular famine was not due to crop failure: it was due to the machinations of businessmen who had managed to create a corner in rice. They bought up the whole crop, stored it in 'godowns', as warehouses are called in India, guarded it with armed Gurkhas, and sat happily on it waiting for the price to rise. They waited just too long.

Good old English Cobbett had this to say:

There is corn in the hands of the corn-dealers; but it surely ought to be in the hands of the farmers . . . Nothing is so sure a sign of national poverty as the absence of stock from the farmer's yard. The corn-stacks are the farmer's strong-box, the landlord's security and the nation's evidence of wealth.

143

These starving millions had been *farmers*. The whole history of mankind since the Neolithic Age has been one of exploitation of the farmers by the townspeople. Here in Bengal, as often before, the townspeople had carried their pillaging just a little bit too far.

The soil of India could probably sustain its present population – *and itself* – but the people would have to go back to the land. They would have to overcome their scruples about killing cattle because half-starved cattle range like a plague over India. They would have to overcome their scruples about killing monkeys. Monkeys eat the crops while human children starve. All right – the monkeys have as much right to live as the children, but it is just as bad for there to be too many monkeys as it is for there to be too many children. The balance of nature should sort this out? But all the leopards and tigers have been eliminated and Man, who should be acting as Viceroy and husbandman here, stays his hand. They would have to stop burning dung: a sin against the Holy Ghost. To burn dung is to burn fertility and starve our Mother the soil. To do this they would have to re-establish forests. They would have to get rid of the grasping landlords and moneylenders. And they would have to relearn the traditional farming of their ancestors.

Then, somehow, they would have to control their propensity for excessive procreation.

Alas alas none of these things are likely to happen. American aid will stave off the very worst for a few more decades – then the moment of truth will come. And as I hear about it I shall remember the agony in the eyes of the father to whom I gave the rupee and who dropped it on the pavement beside him. There may be a surplus of food in India now but there won't be in ten years' time.

We have wandered far, perhaps, from agriculture which is where we started, but it is the nature of organic thinking that knowledge is never divided into thought-proof compartments.

The spectacle of modern so-called 'scientists' sitting each in his little blind box, weighing and measuring and doing silly and often dangerous conjuring tricks, is a pathetic one. True science is not blinkered and takes note of all.

At this moment I am making a transition that I think mankind must make. For seventeen years I owned a farm and was a farmer. Now I am handing the farm over to my children and becoming what the first Man was: a gardener. Or maybe a better word for what I wish to become is the word peasant. The profession of peasant is, I think, the most – indeed perhaps the *only* – honourable one in the world.

I have travelled in true peasant areas about the world and wherever I have come to them I have been bowled over by the sheer beauty of the countryside. I crossed the Elburz Mountains of Iran once, on foot, with a friend, and stayed some days in a valley inhabited by true peasants. I shall never forget the impression of sheer fecundity of that valley. The great spreading mulberry trees were laden with fruit, the little irregular fields of wheat and barley looked delightful between rocky outcrops and stands of oak and other hard woods, in the streams were trout, in the mountains game. I saw no hungry or ill-looking person there and I will never forget the glow of health and beauty of the valley children and the light of fun and love in their eyes. I could hardly be blamed for comparing all this with the disease and hunger and poverty and misery on the one hand, and the gross and unseemly affluence, greed and insolence on the other, of Tehran, the huge city down on the plain. But the valley I am talking about *did not belong to any landlord.* The peasants themselves owned the land.

And wherever I have come to a country husbanded by traditional peasants, practising primarily a subsistence agriculture, and *owning their own land,* I have felt this great sense of beauty and fecundity. Happy is the land where everybody has enough and nobody has too much! *And in which there are not too many people.*

CHAPTER THIRTEEN

I Came to a City

*Man is either Viceroy or else he is an animal that claims special rights
by virtue of its cunning and the devouring efficiency of teeth sharpened
by technological instruments, an animal whose time is up. If he is such
an animal, then he has no rights – he is no more or less than meat – the
elephants and lions, rabbits and mice must in some dim recess of their
being rejoice to see the usurper develop the means of his own
destruction. But if he is Viceroy, then all decay and all trouble in the
created world that surrounds him is in some measure to be laid to his
count . . .
If he is truly what, until recently, he thought he was, then he bears on
his infirm back the burden of creation . . .*
Gai Eaton, *King of the Castle*

AND SO WE COME to the ticklish subject of controlling the
numbers of human beings.

Well of course we can't. We may be able to control the
number of new people we personally bring into the world
(and all I can say here is *mea culpa*) but not one of us can really
have any effect on the numbers of people other people give
rise to. The Catholics say that only God can decide how many
children a family should have and that it is sinful for us wilfully
to limit the numbers – that is if we have sex and of course
nearly all of us do. Cynics say that the Holy Church takes this
stand because it wants to have lots and lots of Catholics and
thus increase the power of the Church and the best way to get

'em is to breed 'em. Those even more cynical (but perhaps more realistic) say that this does not work, really, because very prolific countries are always the poor countries, and therefore the Catholic countries tend to be poorer than the Protestant ones and this does not increase the power of the Church. Considering the matter from the point of view of Nature-not-Man the only conclusion that one can come to is that, although the Catholic countries may be more populous (and by no means all of them are) it is the wealthy Protestant countries that have done, and are doing, most damage to the rest of Nature. There seems to be no doubt that the Reformation was absolutely necessary to clear the way for the kind of empirical science that enables, and the attitude of mind that desires, the 'conquest of nature'.

Protestantism was simply the necessary first stage towards the abandonment of all traditional religion. Whatever one may think about the traditional religions throughout the world – revealed religions they like to call themselves and perhaps they do it with truth – considering them from the point of view of Nature-not-Man (or indeed of Nature, which of course includes Man) one must admit that they tended to a much less destructive, and more harmonious, relationship between Man and the rest of Nature.

The Azorean Catholic fishermen go out in open rowing boats to strike the great whales with the hand-thrown harpoon. It took the Protestant Norwegians to invent the steam and motor whale catchers, the giant factory ship, and the explosive harpoon. It has taken the Japanese (who have utterly abandoned their traditional religion within the course of four decades and plunged holus-bolus into the most Western materialism) to bring in the helicopter as well. The atheistic Russians only lagged behind the Japanese in the terminal slaughter because they were less efficient.

Catholic countries in truth have many children, but it took the Protestant ones to develop medicine to the stage at which most children who are born survive. This development, which must surely seem the most desirable development that has ever happened, in the end will cause (nay is causing already) enormous suffering, both to mankind and to the rest of Nature too. The Japanese murder the whales because they desperately need their meat to survive. The Japanese, before receiving the benefit of 'modern medicine', could (and did) sustain themselves, and well, from what their own islands could produce and from the seas within sailing boat range of their shores. At this very moment there is a Japanese bid to buy the fish dock at Milford Haven, in Wales, to turn it into a fish processing complex. There is not an ocean nor a sea in the world (except a few landlocked ones) with fish in it that hasn't got Japanese fishermen trying to get them out. The Japanese fishing fleets are expanding exponentially, increasing their effectiveness every year, and there is no doubt that they, ably helped by the Poles and the Russians and the good old British, and other 'developed' nations, will exterminate all the edible fish in the sea within a decade or two – if the oil doesn't run out first, for that is the only hope.

Of course, 'babies are more important than fish' – but supposing it so happens that you can't have the first without the second? Supposing there is a limit to the food supply on this planet whatever we do, or no matter how clever the Man in the White Coat is, and that our species is rapidly approaching that limit? What happens then?

The Catholics will say leave it to God. The Protestants will either say exercise self-control, or else use birth control methods. The self-control one is right out I am afraid. *You* or *I* might be able to practise it but then we're exceptional aren't we? (Or at least *you* might be able to practise it.) It just is not going to work. Birth control depends to a certain extent on high technology, which may or may not be going to survive. The pill is almost certainly bad for you. Abortion is disgusting – and it is difficult to refute the charge of murder in

148

connection with it. As I said before I am very good at asking questions but no good at answering them.

Tribal Africans, when I lived among them which I did intimately enough and for long enough to get to know a lot about them, had an answer which worked. Their wives were out of bounds both while they were pregnant and when they were suckling, and they suckled each infant for up to three years! During this period their husbands didn't even share their sleeping mats – they tended to share their mats with their own children or other peoples'. Anyway, it worked, and the population in the bush remained pretty static and there was enough land, and food, for everybody.

Now, of course, with increasing contact with Western ideas, this faultless method of birth control is going, nay has practically gone; and Africa is becoming more and more dependent on imported grain. The population of the continent is zooming, and anybody but a blind man can see that terrible disaster lies ahead. No don't worry – the starving millions of the Third World will *not* overwhelm us fat Westerners. Starving people don't overwhelm anybody. They just quietly starve. I saw it all happening on Chowringee. We inmates of the United Services Club were perfectly safe.

We are told that the Chinese have managed to stabilise their population, for limited periods anyway. It is said that more prosperous peoples have fewer children. In any case Europe and North America are not overpopulated by any real standard. If the people in those areas were more spread out, if they were skilled at survival in the countryside, if the land were more equitably divided, and – above all – if the will to do it were there, twice the existing human populations of these lands could live in decent prosperity, embellishing and husbanding the rest of Nature, and not leaning heavily on it or destroying it at all.

But how could such a result ever be achieved? Can you imagine saying to a bunch of rampaging skinheads: 'Come to the country, work like hell for five years on somebody else's land for next to nothing, then you will be able to take over a piece of land of your own and thereafter earn your own bread in the sweat of your brow!' I wish I could offer a prize for the best entry in a competition for what their replies would be likely to be.

As long as we Westerners continue in our purely nihilistic and anti-traditional beliefs there is just no way that we can arrest our present course, which will inevitably bring all Life on this planet to destruction. What can we do about it? Well I don't know what *we* can do about it because each one of us has free will and I cannot make your mind up for you. But I do know what *I* can do about it. I can change my own mind – get my own head straight. I can ask you to do the same.

If we genuinely believed that *we were still part of Nature* all the rest would follow. If the Japanese genuinely believed that, how could they allow their industrialists to go on to destroy the last whale – to ravage the last fishing ground – to turn the last of the world's forest into chipboard? If the Japanese had stuck to their Shinto-Buddhist traditions they could have done none of these things. If the Europeans had stuck to their Catholic Christian traditions there would have been no Age of Reason – no Industrial Revolution – no Technological Revolution – no atom bomb – no Windscale or Three Mile Island or Chernobyl either. If Ifs and Ands were Pots and Pans there'd be no need for Tinkers!

We have to start from where we are though.

I am (almost) certain that we cannot convince people to believe again that Man is a part of Nature. But I am quite certain that we must try. I would humbly ask the reader to look again at the verse of the *Bhagavad Gita* that I have placed before Chapter 12 of this book.

Meanwhile, apart from trying to persuade people to believe that they are what they obviously are (animals, but viceregal ones) what can we do ourselves to act as if we really believe we are still a part of Nature and do not wish to help Mankind to commit suicide?

Well, try to live as simply and unexploitatively as we can. Try to move to the country where our food does not have to be taken so far to us from where it is grown. Try to grow as much ourselves as we can. Try to buy, as far as possible, food that has been grown organically – that is without heavy chemical inputs.

Try to avoid buying goods that we know are the product of Life-damaging activities. Boycott Japanese goods until the Japanese at least give up whaling, and somehow let the Japanese know you are doing this. Support the 'Green Movement' wherever it is to be found.

These examples of what we can do seem so feeble and so marginal when considered beside the awful problems that loom over us.

Is it already too late? Can we get out of the Black Hole into which, in our blindness, we have led all Life on this planet?

Alas this wretched author does not have a hot-line to that other Author who alone knows the answers to these questions. We can only do what we can do, but that we *must* do – and we must do it for the right reason – because it is right, not because we think it is going to succeed. Only if we do it for that reason will our doing of it be effective.

Did the captain and crew of the *Rainbow Warrior*, the little ship that belonged to Greenpeace, really think they could save a single whale by steaming down to the Antarctic ice and interposing their bodies in tiny rubber dinghies between the ruthless whalers and their prey? *They did it because they knew it was right to do it* and for no other reason.

When I was in India once I was part of an audience that was addressed by an old man – a famous old man – who had spent his life walking around the subcontinent trying to persuade the big landlords to give some of their land to the landless people. I asked him what success he had had. 'None whatever,' was his reply. 'I am like a man trying to demolish a brick wall with his head. So far I have not succeeded in even knocking some dust off the wall. But I shall go on doing it for the rest of my life *because I know it is right to do it.*'

And who knows if his actions will not, one day, prevail after all? But that is not the point. His motive for doing what he did was that he knew it was right to do it – not because he thought he could succeed.

And, surely, this is the sort of faith we have got to exhibit today.

We have *got* to hurl our bodies in front of the bulldozers! We must make it absolutely clear to the despoilers and destroyers that if we cannot ultimately stop them at least we will try – with our minds – our bodies – our souls – and our wits! And who knows? We are fewer now than they are, and much poorer; but we have weapons that they lack completely – we have sharp intelligence (not just low cunning which we must concede to them), we have poetry, humour and wit. Laughter is one of our sharp weapons – we must use it like a rapier.

We must work incessantly at breaking up the gross and swollen 'nation-states'. (Leopold Kohr's book *The Breakdown of Nations* and Papworth's *New Politics* are enormously helpful at understanding this. No man should call himself civilised unless he has read one or both of these.) Perhaps nothing else good can be achieved until this is achieved: in nations that are too big to be comprehended by the human mind no real progress towards sanity can be made. Countries – cities – business – all human institutions must be broken down to units of an humane size: a size that the ordinary human mind and soul can grasp.

And whether the hand that rocks the cradle rules the world or not at least we know that the fingers that dip into the purse rule the economy. The Campaign for Real Ale showed what can be done here. Even the giant national breweries have been forced to put up a show of producing 'real ale' though their so-called real ale is no more real ale than the fizzy stuff they sold before, but what has been achieved is the salvation of dozens of small local breweries which were on the point of closing down. If the Real Ale Campaigners tire not in their efforts they may bring the great national breweries to bankruptcy and that would be marvellous. And now a Real Bread Campaign has started in England. May it revive the family baker and destroy the wrapped-pap factories.

Boycott as far as we can all huge companies and multi-nationals. Support local industries. Because it stupidly let itself be drawn into the E.E.C., Ireland has to allow floods of foreign goods in to the utter destruction of its own industries. Its government has now had the sense to try to correct this by funding a massive 'Buy Irish' campaign. This doesn't seem to stop the country from being absolutely flooded with foreign goods. Irish men and women line up in the dole queues to get the money to buy goods *that they should be growing or making themselves.* One expects this sort of *bêtise* in a big country – it is sad when it happens in a small one, but Ireland has bartered away the advantages of being small by joining in a larger lunacy.

We must make it absolutely clear to the stupid people who rule our swollen 'nation-states' that we will make their work as difficult as we can for them. We will help them only when they work on the side of Life – when they work on the side of death, as they do nearly all the time, we will oppose them all the way.

We will make it as difficult as we can for them to pile up their megadeaths, to build their poisoning power plants, to bury their radioactive filth in our beautiful mountains or dump it in our seas. We will make it clear to the big industrialists that we do not want their dirty products – we will get back to simple things and return to Adam's cheer again. These people talk endlessly of 'growth'. The growth of what – the growth of the human spirit – of the human soul?

We must get back to our heritage – our birthright – our true charge – the land. We must insist on being allowed to fulfil our trust, to be husbandmen again: lovingly to care for the soil from which all terrestrial life comes and to which it returns.

We must forsake the swollen conurbations that deface our planet and disgrace mankind.

I came to a city. A city that had grown beautifully and organically in a fertile populous plain where children played and laughed and sang in the groves and orchards and gardens, where men and women worked hard and joyously to till the soil. The city started straight from the countryside: no ugly, soulless suburbs. And as I entered the city I wept and trembled with wonder at the beauty of it for the city had been built for the glory of God. But alas – the city was only in my dreams.

When the oil has gone the day of the swollen conurbations (I dare not use the beautiful word *city* in their connection) will crumble and fall. No no – the Nuke will not save them. It is too expensive, too little, and too late. When the Nuke bill finally comes up for payment – when the final demand comes – it will be found that the cost of development, waste storage, waste disposal, compensation of cancer cases, massive protection, special armed police forces and all the rest of it will weigh the scale. All such costs have been carefully excluded from nuclear industry bookkeeping so far – but the bills will still be presented! You can falsify the books but you still have to pay the bill.

No no – the nuke is not going to save the conurbations. Nothing – nothing – is going to take the place of a power that gushes out of the earth wherever somebody drills a hole in the right place.

And, with no or extremely expensive oil, and no petrochemicals, farmers will have to produce vast quantities of food, with hardly any labour because labour has priced itself out of the market, and the food has got to be carried huge distances – often halfway round the world – and processed, and stored, and distributed to a hundred billion city parasites who have nothing worthwhile to give in exchange.

No, *H. extinctor*, the whole thing is due to come crashing down and not all the Men in White Coats in the world will save it – no matter how much money they are given to throw at the problems.

We must start now – now – *now* working for a new organic order – a new harmony – a new dream. 'For the world is a dream that is dying, or one that is coming to birth.'

D.H. Lawrence wrote that Mankind is like a great uprooted tree with its roots in the air. We must get right way up again and strike our roots down into the soil. We must plant ourselves again in the Universe.

It is almost as though Mankind were splitting into two species. *H. extinctor* and *Homo* . . . what? *Man the Husbandman* is good enough for me. *Sapiens* is far too arrogant and distant from the truth. Man the Husbandman – Latin that.

And we must become a whole people again.

We must break away from the macho dream – it has turned out to be a nightmare. Women should be women and have womanly qualities and men should be men, but they should complement each other and neither sex should dominate. People of each sex should bring their wisdom and intuition and strength to the great task of serving the Life Force. The Life Force, *God* if you like it that way, is neither male nor female.

We need the equal influence of women again in the world. No woman would build up megadeaths, or dream up machines to take fools to the stars. Those are the mad sick dreams of arrogant males. What – go and pollute other stars when we have made such a mess of this one? Ruin this one first so that we may go and ruin the others?

No, let us, women and men, start humbly and diligently to turn *this* planet into the garden that the Bible tells us it was before the Fall, when 'God put the man and woman in the garden to dress it and keep it'.

The world a garden. That is the destiny wished for us, I believe, by the Life Force.

The New Kurukshetra – the Battle between Good and Evil – is about to be joined on this planet and my heart tells me, against all odds, the forces of Life will win. No doubt as the enemy plunges to destruction he will take a lot of the living with him, and a lot of the Life on our little planet will be destroyed, but my heart tells me, even if my head does not, that some Life will survive, and maybe even some of our form of Life.

Life is tough and resiliant and has withstood great cataclysms before. I know there must be Life on other planets – on many millions of them. Probably the thin, tenuous, green film around this little globe matters very little in cosmic terms at all.

But it matters to me, and – sister, brother – it matters to you – sister wren, brother whale, sister grass, brother worm, Mother Earth.

resurgence

FOR A GREEN PERSPECTIVE

Green Books grew out of *Resurgence* magazine, which was started in 1966 to promote the philosophy of small is beautiful and care for the planet Earth. If you would like to regularly read the work of distinguished writers who have a vision of wholeness, why not take out a subscription to *Resurgence?*

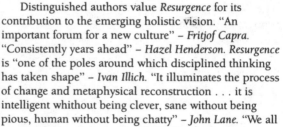

At *Resurgence* we believe in the wonder of nature and the good that should flow from it; we believe in art, culture and the good things in life; more than anything we believe that humanity has a future and that the shape of this future lies in our own hands.

Resurgence is a friendly magazine; it does not dwell on the negative or on gloom and doom. Every edition is packed with 60 pages of articles, book reviews, photographs, Business Diary, Letter from America and poetry. It covers issues of development disarmament, health, education, science, appropriate technology and human scale in all manner of organisations.

Distinguished authors value *Resurgence* for its contribution to the emerging holistic vision. "An important forum for a new culture" – *Fritjof Capra.* "Consistently years ahead" – *Hazel Henderson. Resurgence* is "one of the poles around which disciplined thinking has taken shape" – *Ivan Illich.* "It illuminates the process of change and metaphysical reconstruction . . . it is intelligent whithout being clever, sane without being pious, human without being chatty" – *John Lane.* "We all try to grab for *Resurgence* when it arrives" – *Jay Walljasper,* Executive Editor of Utne Reader (USA). "When I am looking for inspiration I read *Resurgence*" – *Gerard Morgan-Grenville.*

If you read *Resurgence* you are in good company with many distinguished writers. They include: *Wendell Berry, Fritjof Capra, Hazel Henderson, Ivan Illich, Jonathon Porritt, Laurens van der Post, Kathleen Raine, James Robertson, John Seymour, Rupert Sheldrake, Gary Snyder, James Lovelock.*

We believe that once you have read *Resurgence* you will want to be a regular subscriber. For this reason we will send you two back issues of *Resurgence* completely free on receipt of your cheque for one year's subscription. If you don't like the look, the feel and the content of these sample issues of the magazine, write to us and we will refund your payment in full.

Please send your cheque for £14.00 to: Resurgence, Salem Cottage, Trelill, Bodmin, Cornwall PL30 3HZ.